Bowhunting Big Game

Bowhunting Big Game

Hunter's Information Series™
North American Hunting Club
Minneapolis, Minnesota

Bowhunting Big Game

Copyright © 1993, North American Hunting Club

Library of Congress Catalog Card Number 92-62494
ISBN 0-914697-53-6

Printed in U.S.A.
2   3   4   5   6   7   8   9

The North American Hunting Club
offers a line of hats for hunters.
For information, write:
North American Hunting Club
P.O. Box 3401
Minneapolis, MN 55343

Contents

Acknowledgments

The North American Hunting Club would like to thank everyone who helped create this book.

Artist David Rottinghaus provided all illustrations. Photos, in addition to the author's, were supplied by Chuck Adams, Todd Amenrud, Bear Archery (of Fred Bear), Easton Aluminum (of Doug Easton), Brad Harris, Mark Kayser, Myles Keller, *North American Hunter* Publisher Mark LaBarbera, Managing Editor of Books Ron Larsen, Peter Mathieson, Len Rue Jr. and the Pope and Young Club. Providing information were J. R. Absher, Chuck Adams, G. Fred Asbel, Wayne Carlton, Judd Cooney, Craig Dougherty, Jim Dougherty, Bob Fratzke, Brad Harris, Earl Hoyt, M. R. James, Owen Jeffrey, Myles Keller, Norb Mullaney, Terry Ragsdale, Eddie Salter, Rick Sapp, Chuck Saunders, Jim Schlender, Randy Schoeck, Dwight Schuh, Frank Scott and Ev Tarrell.

A special thanks to the North American Hunting Club's publications staff for all their efforts: Publisher Mark LaBarbera, Managing Editor of Books Ron Larsen, Associate Editor of Books Colleen Ferguson and Editorial Assistant Victoria Brouillette. Thanks also to Vice President of Product Marketing Mike Vail, Assistant Vice President/ Marketing Manager Cal Franklin and Marketing Project Coordinator Laura Resnik.

About The Author

Dan Dietrich isn't your everyday bowhunter. He is a student of the sport, having learned to make a compound bow and arrows from cedar shafts. He will dig until he finds the right answer, and he isn't afraid to call on leading authorities for their expertise. As senior editor for the *North American Hunter* magazine, Dan directs a stellar list of Bowhunting Advisory Council members: Chuck Adams, M. R. James, Jim Dougherty and Judd Cooney—all big names in modern bowhunting. In addition, Dan has gained Associate Member status in bowhunting's prestigious Pope and Young Club by taking three record-book quality big-game animals during hunting trips throughout the United States and parts of Canada.

Dan's love of hunting grew out of his outdoor experiences as a youth on and around the Mississippi River's backwaters near the old river town of Red Wing, Minnesota. During the 1970s Dan studied at Red Wing's Environmental Learning Center (ELC), one of the few educational facilities in the country dedicated to enriching young people's lives by teaching them outdoor crafts and skills. In ELC's archery program, Dan learned about bows, arrows and bowhunting.

As a graduate of the ELC, Dan stayed on for a fifth year as an instructor-naturalist, then worked as an ELC field instructor. He led young adults on kayaking, cave exploring and other outdoor adventures. Moving on to the University of Wisconsin-Stevens Point (UWSP), Dan found time to hunt upland birds and white-tailed deer.

After receiving a bachelor's degree in communications at USWP, Dan joined the *North American Hunter* staff as associate editor in 1988, and was named senior editor in 1991.

Dan has bowhunted across North America for pronghorns, elk, mule deer, black bear and, of course, white-tailed deer. He also enjoys gun hunting, and competitive field archery. A field-archery highlight for him was competing in the Desert Shootout tournament in Tucson, Arizona, drawing back with the likes of Olympic Gold Medal winner Jay Barr, renown bow designer Tom Jennings and PSE President Pete Shepley whose firm sponsors the tournament. In addition, Dan has shared his bowhunting knowledge and experience with television viewers on the NAHC television show, "North American Outdoors," which is seen on ESPN.

An award-winning writer and photographer, Dan is a member of both the Outdoor Writers Association of America and the Association of Great Lakes Outdoor Writers. He and his wife, Kari, live in Old Frontenac, Minnesota.

Dedication

A t the Environmental Learning Center (ELC) in Red Wing, Minnesota, I learned to build log cabins and kayaks, trap beaver and shoot bows and arrows. Few schools teach such fundamental outdoor skills today. Bruce Ause, ELC's director and fellow bowhunter, introduced me to bowhunting, and he is the person who first encouraged me to write about and photograph outdoor experiences. For this, Bruce, I am forever grateful.

Foreword

North American Hunting Club Members rank among the most avid and successful outdoorsmen anywhere in the world. They hunt with modern rifles, handguns and shotguns, blackpowder firearms, bows, crossbows, falcons and about any other legal method you can imagine. Putting it frankly, NAHC Members love hunting in all its shapes and forms.

But within that broad spectrum, each of us has a favorite; for every NAHC Member there is likely one special niche, one special place, one favorite kind of hunting. There are numerous reasons for particular favorites. Regardless of the reasons, the NAHC has long stood to help each of its Members enjoy their favorites even more.

This book, *Bowhunting Big Game*, is written for and dedicated to those NAHC Members who enjoy the challenges and fun of hunting with a bow.

As much as firearms hunters might deny it, there is indeed a special challenge in hunting with a stick, string and arrows. That challenge is getting within spitting distance of wary game, such as a trophy white-tailed buck, a bugling bull elk or a strutting gobbler. And it's that particular challenge that makes bowhunting so addicting to those who seriously try it.

Things seem to happen when you are bowhunting that never would when you're afield with a rifle or shotgun. Maybe it's a hawk roosting not more than 20 feet above your tree stand. Maybe it's a

squirrel that brushes your pants cuff or a song bird that lands on your nocked arrow. Maybe it's that shiver you get when you're leaving the woods after dark and a coyote yaps just on the other side of the ridge. For those outdoors people who love it and live it, there is no denying that bowhunting is something special.

Whether you look at bowhunting as a way to extend your hunting time or as an all-consuming hunting challenge, *Bowhunting Big Game* has much to offer. It's written by a man who loves bowhunting.

As NAHC President, I'm proud to tell you about the author of this book. Dan Dietrich joined the NAHC staff right out of school. He came aboard as an associate editor for NAHC publications and edited many of the previous titles in the Hunter's Information Series. In-depth, hands-on experience endowed Dan with a sixth-sense for what NAHC Members want in their Club publications.

At the same time, Dan quickly developed a love—make that a passion—for bowhunting. It wasn't long before he took over as coordinator of the prestigious NAHC Bowhunting Advisory Council to oversee the work of legendary bowhunting figures like Chuck Adams, Jim Dougherty, Dwight Schuh, Norb Mullaney and Judd Cooney! Dan has become one of the fastest rising young stars of the bowhunting world. In just a few seasons he has put three animals in the Pope and Young Club record book; one of his pronghorns ranks among the top 25 percent ever taken with a bow!

In commissioning Dan, now senior editor, to write *Bowhunting Big Game*, we called on him to pull it all together. We asked him to share the best advice of the legendary NAHC Bowhunting Advisory Council members, the counsel of the industry's leading equipment manufacturers and researchers and his own fresh perspective on this ancient sport. That's just what he did.

NAHC Members who want to relive the thrills of their greatest bowhunts, learn how to improve their skills and make hunting even more enjoyable or spend more priceless hours afield pursuing hunting's greatest challenges won't be able to put *Bowhunting Big Game* down.

We're proud to introduce you to bowhunter Dan Dietrich. And we're equally proud to exclusively publish this exciting Hunter's Information Series edition.

Enjoy ... and good hunting.

Steven F. Burke
President
North American Hunting Club

1

The Bowhunting Experience

Having skimped and saved two years for his first guided big-game bowhunt, Bob Atwill finally saw his special savings account top $3,000. He had worked overtime, stayed home most weekends and lived on a tight budget.

During the long winter months, Bob planned his dream bowhunt. Knowing that he wanted to hunt elk and mule deer, he attended a regional sport show where he talked with numerous Western outfitters. At the show he narrowed his choices to six potential outfitters. Then, at home, he called the references provided by the outfitters on his list. Next, following a friend's advice, Bob called the state game departments to reaffirm that each outfitter was licensed and in good standing. He also talked with state game biologists about elk and mule deer populations in specific areas. He compared this information with what the outfitters provided.

After talking over his options with his wife and hunting buddies, Bob booked a September elk and mule deer bowhunt with a Colorado outfitter. The outfitter specialized in horseback, remote wilderness hunts in southern Colorado's San Juan Mountains. This would be a 2-on-1 hunt—meaning Bob and another hunter would have the same guide. The outfitter's price for the 7-day hunt was $1,750. Combining this with licenses, transportation and equipment, Bob expected spending between $2,500 and $3,000. He would also use half of his annual vacation.

During that spring and summer, Bob hiked and biked. Because this would be a high country hunt at elevations reaching 10,000 feet above sea level, Bob needed to be in top physical condition. He also shot his bow twice a week—Wednesday after work and early Saturday morning. Following his guide's recommended equipment list, Bob began setting out his gear more than a month before the hunt. Of course, September couldn't arrive soon enough.

But eventually it did.

On September 13, Bob flew to Durango, Colorado. The outfitter met him at the airport. They stopped at a local sporting goods store so Bob could buy his nonresident archery deer and elk licenses. That evening, Bob met the other three hunters and the other guide at the ranch. The seventh man who was the camp cook, horse wrangler and Jack-of-all-trades already was at base camp keeping hungry grizzly bears at bay, they joked.

The early morning light silhouetted the mountain peaks as a pack train of 10 horses wound its way up into the San Juan Mountains. Not only was this Bob's first Western big-game bowhunt, but it was his first ride on a horse. It took most of the morning before he settled into the rhythm of his assigned steed. All in all, it was a most pleasant, relaxing day.

The sun was just above the mountainous horizon to the west when they arrived at base camp—one cook tent and two sleeping tents. The group unloaded their gear and unpacked their bows. The four hunters practiced shooting and compared equipment. Over a hearty supper they talked with the guides about tomorrow morning's hunt and their hopes for success.

The guides explained where and how they would hunt. The hunters were told what to do if one of them downed a buck or bull, and what to do in the event of an emergency. The guides also reiterated that this was a 4-point-minimum area—meaning only bulls with four points or more on one side or cows were legal. Because this was Bob's first elk bowhunt, he immediately told his guide that he would take any legal bull. And if he hadn't taken a bull by the last day, he would take any legal elk. He would hunt deer only if the elk hunting proved terrible or if he harvested an elk early in the hunt.

At 4 o'clock the next morning, Bob, a second hunter and their guide rode out of base camp. Winning the coin toss at camp, Bob hunted with the guide the first day. The other hunter would post over a wallow and then hunt with the guide on the second day. The three rode in the dark through mountain passes and along spring-fed creeks. An hour before sunrise they tied up the horses, dropped off

After two years of planning, scrimping and saving, Bob Atwill finally had been able to experience a situation like this on the slopes of Colorado's San Juan mountains during his own dream hunt.

the other hunter near the wallow and walked toward a string of open meadows.

Just before sunrise the guide located a bugling bull. They stalked through the woods and set up on the edge of a meadow as the sun crested the horizon. Bob hunkered down in a pine tree's shadow; his guide was about 10 yards behind him. In the early morning light they could see the bull and his cow harem in the meadow. After peering through binoculars, the guide gave Bob the thumbs-up sign—meaning it was a legal bull and to shoot if the opportunity arose. The guide also held up six fingers, and mouthed the words ''six by six.''

Bob's heart began thumping as he nocked an arrow. This was more exciting than he had anticipated for this early in the hunt.

The guide's bugle pierced the mountain valley's stillness. But while that bugle echoed off the mountain walls, the six-by-six responded with his own bugle.

In less than 10 minutes, the guide had managed to bring the bull to their edge of the field. The bull came straight toward the bugle's sound and stood facing Bob. He estimated the distance to be only 25 yards.

When the bull looked to one side searching for the challenger, Bob drew his bow and laid the 30-yard pin on the bull's chest.

The bull then turned and walked broadside. Bob knew he had to wait for the bull to stop before he could shoot. As he waited, he looked at the bull's rack. It was huge, especially compared to the white-tailed deer back home. This was the first bull elk he had ever seen or heard bugle. And it would be the first bull elk he would shoot. Bob was already wondering whether this trophy's shoulder mount would fit in the living room.

Just then his guide ''cow talked.'' The bull stopped and, in that instant, Bob settled a pin behind the front shoulder and released.

His first thought after the release was of the rack. He glanced at the rack but then his eye caught a flash of his arrow's orange fletch. Immediately Bob felt a twinge of regret. The arrow was too high and too far back! He even leaned to the side like a bowler hoping to bring the ball back into the strike zone, but the arrow had sailed over the bull's back into the meadow.

Unscathed, the bull turned and charged back toward his harem. The cows, sensing his urgency, trotted off in front of him. With their hooves thumping the mountain meadow floor, Bob could only stare at them and whisper a profanity under his breath … his guide was silent.

Bob had just missed his chance at a bull elk on the first day of his first guided big-game bowhunt. Unfortunately, he would not get an-

Bowhunter numbers continue to increase in North America, partly because more and more gun hunters are taking up bows. Longer seasons, special archery-only hunting and less hunting pressure are some of the reasons.

other opportunity. He returned home empty-handed to his family and friends with only a story and memories.

Intrinsic Reasons For Bowhunting's Growth

Compared to hunters who use handguns, rifles, shotguns and muzzleloaders, bowhunters have the lowest success rate on big game. A 27-state survey found that bowhunter success on white-tailed deer averaged 14 percent; gun hunters averaged 35.

The reason for this difference is fairly academic. Accurate shots can be made by firearms hunters out to 400 yards; bowhunters typically average about a distance of 20 yards for a killing shot. A deer hunter's .30-06 clips along at 2,800 feet per second (fps), or more than twice the speed of sound. A bowhunter's arrow trots out at a maximum of 230 fps. Therefore, a bullet always will arrive before the sound of the shot, but an arrow never will.

Despite these limitations and the fact that only one hunter in seven will take a deer, some three million bowhunters take to the woods and fields each year. They don their camouflage, grab their bows and slip silently into the woods hoping that today will be the day when a wary whitetail, lumbering black bear or some other big-game animal will mosey within 20 yards of their tree stand. But why? What is it about bowhunting that instills such admirable patience and persistence? Why did the number of bowhunters in North America jump by 28 percent in a five-year period?

Perhaps it is the challenge, nostalgia and satisfaction of using a bow. The challenge, as noted bowhunter Chuck Adams says, is to get within "eyelash batting range" of the game animal. To do that a hunter must fully understand game behavior and pinpoint the animal's home turf. A bowhunter must also slip into that area and set up undetected, and remain undetected until the animal comes within range. Then draw back, aim and release without alerting the animal. And even then, as Bob Atwill will tell you, it's not a sure thing. That is the challenge.

"I bowhunt first and foremost for the challenge," says Adams, one of the nation's most succcessful bowhunters. "That's why I switched from gun hunting years ago. I intensely enjoy every aspect of bowhunting. I enjoy being out in the animal's natural state and learning about it. But, first and foremost, getting within eyelash batting range of animals and getting an accurate shot is why I bowhunt." Adams is the first bowhunter to take all 27 recognized North American big-game animals.

Or it could be something more romantic, even nostalgic. According to the late Fred Bear in *The Archers Bible*, " ... many historians agree that these three innovations (discovery of fire, the invention of the wheel and the principle of the bow and arrow) were the chief factors in man's rise above his fellow creatures. In those early days, and indeed for many centuries, the bow was a tool of grim necessity in obtaining food and winning battles. As the romantic sport of the ages, archery still appeals to man's atavistic instincts. It gives him the chance to subconsciously relive the days of his forebears who conquered enemies and sustained life with little elsc than their wits and their bows and arrows."

It could also be the satisfaction bowhunting brings. Dwight Schuh, a 20-year veteran and leading authority on back-country big-game bowhunts, says, "The reason I bowhunt is that it suits my basic personality. That's just the way I like to do things. I've always liked the wilderness. I like hard, physical exercise. I like discovering and pioneering. And bowhunting in isolated places, trying to discover

Chuck Adams, probably the best known bowhunter in America, says he bowhunts "first and foremost for the challenge." That's why he switched from gun hunting to bowhunting years ago.

new areas, satisfies those personality traits in me.''

Practical Reasons For Bowhunting's Growth

Hunting season always seems too far away and too short. Bow-hunting can extend your time afield and open a smorgasbord of hunting opportunities. Bowhunters typically enjoy longer hunting seasons than their firearms counterparts. In Minnesota, for example, the archery deer season runs 105 days—from mid-September to the end of December. The state's firearms deer season lasts four days in one region and up to 16 days in the others. No matter how early in the morning you cook the eggs and bacon, it's difficult to cram a full year's worth of big-game hunting enjoyment into a four- or 16-day season. That situation can be especially frustrating for NAHC Members who hunt an average of 56 days per year.

Comparing archery and firearms deer seasons in 27 states shows why bowhunting provides more opportunities in most states.

Granted, not every state offers longer archery seasons, but 19 of them do. And in those states, bowhunters can often hunt before, during and after the rut. Plus, the longer seasons mean that a thunderstorm or cold front will only ruin a weekend, not the entire hunting season.

Despite these longer seasons, however, bowhunters are still less than half as successful as firearms deer hunters. According to the deer harvest summaries from those same states, one in seven (14 percent) bowhunters took home a deer; one in three firearms hunters (35 percent) was successful. Bowhunter success ranged from 3 percent (Maine and New Hampshire) to 36.5 percent (Georgia). Gun-hunter success ranged from 7.4 percent (Vermont) to 96 percent (Georgia).

Another reason for bowhunting is the special archery-only hunts. As North America's urban populations grow and spread into the suburbs, former "wild" areas within commuting distances of major cities now support schools, homes and businesses ... and the ever-adaptable white-tailed deer.

In some suburbs, deer populations grow and eventually exceed the area's carrying capacity. The result is an increase in the number of deer/vehicle accidents as deer move about in search of food. Suburbs faced with this dilemma will often open special archery-only hunts. Bows are quiet and have a short effective range, making them the tool of choice in areas where firearms discharge could be disturbing or perceived as dangerous.

Bowhunters also have the opportunity to hunt undisturbed game. During a firearms deer season in Wisconsin, a hunting buddy and I

Comparing Bow And Gun Seasons

State	Bow Season	Gun Season
Alabama	108 days	75 days
Arkansas	151 days	30 days
Connecticut	61 days	30 days
Delaware	113 days	10 days
Florida	30 days	72 days
Georgia	35 days	57-79 days
Kentucky	109 days	10 days
Louisiana	112 days	60 days
Maine	25 days	25 days
Maryland	80 days	7 days
Massachusetts	18 days	6-9 days
Minnesota	105 days	4-16 days
Mississippi	53 days	47 days
Missouri	83 days	9 days
New Hampshire	93 days	26 days
New Jersey	76 days	6-8 days
New York	23-40 days	23-44 days
North Carolina	24-54 days	12-67 days
Oklahoma	73 days	9 days
Pennsylvania	46 days	13-16 days
Rhode Island	120 days	9 days
South Carolina	10 days	60-140 days
Tennessee	22-33 days	12-34 days
Texas	30 days	65 days
Virginia	25-55 days	12-42 days
Vermont	32 days	16 days
West Virginia	67 days	12 days

As this chart indicates, many states offer archery seasons that are appreciably longer than firearms seasons. Most dramatic example is Minnesota's 105-day bow season, compared with the state's four- to 16-day gun seasons.

discovered that when several thousand gun hunters enter the woods on opening day, the deer quickly learn to no longer walk from feeding to bedding areas on familiar paths. The deer changed their habits quickly and completely. Our pre-season scouting efforts didn't do much good because the deer were gone—headed for the thickest, densest cover.

The next year, however, we hunted the deer that had taken cover in the middle of the swamp—the only place where most hunters wouldn't bother checking. We bagged a buck on one of the tiny islands within the swamp that year.

Bowhunters typically aren't faced with this sudden change in behavior. With an earlier season and fewer hunters in the woods, chances are good that scouting reveals behavior patterns that most likely will not change by opening morning.

Also, it is often easier to secure a nonresident archery tag than a nonresident firearms tag. In some states, nonresident archery tags are over-the-counter purchases, while nonresident firearms tags are not even available.

South Dakota's pronghorn herd was devastated by winter kill in the mid-1980s. The state closed archery and firearms hunting to all nonresidents. After several years, the pronghorn herd began its comeback. The state then opened the pronghorn season to nonresident bowhunters who submitted an application. South Dakota's pronghorn herd has rebounded to the point where nonresident firearms tags are available again.

Finally, bowhunting is a natural transition for gun hunters. The same skills are required for both bowhunting and firearms hunting. In fact, many bowhunters hunt with a firearm also. Similarly, most gun hunters enjoy bowhunting.

The Best Path To Successful Bowhunting

Every method of hunting offers its challenges and rewards. Bowhunting, however, by its inherent limitations, boosts the challenge another notch. Scouting, stand selection, bow selection, bow tuning, camouflage, scent management and shot placement are all elements that must fit together in order for the bowhunter to achieve success.

Bowhunting requires common sense, attention to detail and some bowhunting knowledge.

"The knowledge that's available today can make you a much better bowhunter, faster and with fewer mistakes," says Judd Cooney, a bowhunting veteran since 1954. "Back then the information wasn't available. We didn't know about the value of tree stands. We didn't know about deer trails. We didn't know about scrapes and rattling. If I could go back with the hunting knowledge I have now, I would kill a huge buck every year. There's no question about it."

This book provides the advice, opinions and perceptions of today's leading bowhunters—the ones who have learned from patience and perseverance. They share their thoughts on hunting strategies, bow selection, scouting tactics, practice techniques and more. Who are these experts? They include Chuck Adams, who has taken 38 Pope and Young Club record-book animals; Myles Keller, a 30-year bowhunting veteran and whitetail bowhunter with 18 official P&Y record-book whitetails; Dwight Schuh, the leading authority on back-country big-game bowhunts with more than 20 years of bowhunting experience; Terry Ragsdale, three-time world archery champion and four-time National Field Archery Association champion; Bob Fratzke, 30-year bowhunting veteran who has harvested 24 trophy-class whitetails, and G. Fred Asbel, the president of bowhunting's P&Y Club and a bowhunter for more than 30 years.

Many reasons exist for bowhunting's rapid growth. The most important one, perhaps, is that it brings us back to the natural world in a more intimate way. It allows hunters to better understand and appreciate the wild, helping them become better hunters. According to

In some cases nonresident archery permits are easier to obtain than nonresident firearms permits. The author, hunting as a nonresident, bagged this pronghorn in South Dakota. At the time only nonresident archery permits were available.

Ruth Rudner, *Parabola* writer, ''To enter the world where the wild is at home, and where success—however one measures it—depends on the hunter's ability to be at home as well, is to claim our birthright to wildness. Hunter and hunted are partners, the presence of each honing the instincts and senses of the other. The hunter possesses the skills to chase; the hunted the skills to evade. Each provides the other with an energy necessary for life.''

Few things in today's world can create the excitement and the flow of adrenalin that successfully outwitting a creature of the wild can for a bowhunter. Approaching a big-game animal to within striking distance undetected provides a feeling of accomplishment that will continue to live with a bowhunter—even if the attempt to take the animal proves unsuccessful. And the constant reminder of the beauty and, sometimes, stark reality of nature is but frosting on the cake.

2

History Of Modern Bowhunting

Bowhunting history dates back thousands of years to the early history of man. At some point in time, somebody tied a string to a stick and shot the world's first arrow. The world was changed forever.

Wayne C. McKinney, in his 1966 book, *Archery*, wrote: "From the artifacts such as arrow points and tools, [archery historians] generally agree that man started using crude archery tackle 10,000 to 20,000 years ago." McKinney reported the oldest bow in existence dates back to 2,000 B.C.

In the book *The Archer's Bible*, the late Fred Bear wrote: "The bow has been extremely important in man's inheritance. Many nations, in fact whole civilizations—among them, the Egyptians, Sumerians, Greeks, Romans, Babylonians, Syrians, Turks, Persians, Arabians, Mongols, Chinese and Japanese—were largely built or destroyed on flights of humming arrow shafts."

Although the bows most bowhunters use today possess the refinements and improvements brought about during the past 50 years, bows and arrows have a history dating back much farther than most of us could have ever imagined.

The Source Of Modern Bowhunting

Even though bowhunting's roots are from years ago, it remains the most primitive form of hunting still practiced. And yet, modern bowhunting is a high-tech proposition. Risers are machined from

Thanks to Ishi, the last of the Yana Indian tribe, the bowhunting tradition was passed on to Saxon Pope (left) and Art Young who hunted extensively with bows and kept the tradition alive.

solid bars of aluminum. Arrows are made from super straight aluminum or space-age carbon. Eccentrics are designed, tested and refined by sophisticated computer programs. Undoubtedly, this is the modern age of bowhunting. Today's bowhunting tackle can cleanly and efficiently harvest every big-game animal in North America.

However, you may not be reading this book or thinking about bowhunting if it weren't for the Indian Ishi. Honest. In 1911, Ishi walked from the wilderness onto a California farm. He was the last member of the Yana Indian tribe.

Settlers already had spread throughout the American West, bringing a new and more effective hunting tool: guns and gun powder. Guns became the tool of choice for gathering food and waging war. By the early 1900s, the bow, which had been such a mainstay of the American Indian's way of life, had been abandoned.

Ishi and a handful of his tribe, however, lived deep in the California woods. They avoided contact with the modern world and continued their native way of handcrafting bows, arrows and broadheads, as well as bowhunting.

After banner headlines about the last "wild" Indian walking out of the woods, Ishi moved to a University and met Saxon Pope. Ishi

Bowhunting received a major push from the efforts of the late Fred Bear who studied under Art Young and is credited with lifting bowhunting out of the Stone Age into the Modern Age.

Doug Easton, shown with a nice mule deer buck taken with the long bow, was one of the pioneers of modern bowhunting. He developed and produced the first aluminum arrow, and became the world's leading arrow manufacturer.

had walked out of the wilderness and into the modern world, but he brought with him the bowhunting history of his tribe. Ishi passed on the bowhunting tradition to Saxon Pope. Saxon Pope passed it on to Art Young. And Pope and Young hunted extensively with bows and arrows.

In 1923, Pope published the book, *Hunting With The Bow And Arrow*, which described bowhunting and examined the construction of bows and arrows. It is credited as a force in sparking real interest in bowhunting.

In 1927, Fred Bear saw Art Young's film, *Alaska Adventures*. The two met and began building archery equipment and shooting bows together.

In the late 1920s and early 1930s a handful of people were crafting and experimenting with wood bows and arrows. Rawhide was placed on the back of yew bows to give them strength. It was an era when people like Pope, Young, Bear, Earl Hoyt, Doug Easton and Howard Hill discovered their life's passion. It was an era of discovery. There are several bowhunters, I believe, who would swap their modern, high-tech equipment and today's comfortable lifestyle for the chance to sit around a campfire with the young Fred Bear or Saxon Pope. It was a time when a handful of men began to redefine the ancient sport of archery, and set its course for the future.

In the 1940s Easton, who first started building yew bows in 1922

Bowhunters like Chuck Adams have picked up the bowhunting torch. He became the first to take all 27 recognized North American big-game species with a bow. It has put him at the forefront of America's bowhunting fraternity.

The late Fred Bear, founder of the Bear Archery Company and a legend in modern bow-
hunting, is shown with an 810-pound brown bear taken in Alaska during one of Bear's
numerous hunting trips to various parts of the world.

and met Pope in 1924, manufactured the first trademarked aluminum arrow shaft. And in the 1950s a new product called fiberglass was applied to wood bow limbs. The result was a smoother, faster and more durable bow limb. The evolution of modern bowhunting, of course, continues, and is discussed in detail in the following section.

Fred Bear is credited with lifting archery from the Stone Age into the Modern Age. He is, as author John Mitchell described him, ''...the Papa Bear of the great outdoors, the archer emeritus, the patron saint of bowhunting in America, the elder statesman of the field sports.''

According to NAHC President Steve Burke, ''Bowhunting lost its father in 1988 when Fred Bear passed away. Nobody fills a father's shoes. But there is a bowhunter, I think, who is walking a similar path. He's the first bowhunter to complete the North American Super Slam. He has taken more than three-dozen official P&Y record-book animals—more than any other bowhunter. And he has

Modern Bowhunting's History

Modern bowhunting's most important milestones:

1911	Ishi passes on bowhunting tradition to Saxon Pope.
Early 1920s	Saxon Pope and Art Young join forces in keeping bowhunting alive.
1928	Claud Lapp invents compound bow.
1930s	The first take-apart bows are manufactured.
1933	Fred Bear and Charles Piper start Bear Products Company for manufacturing bowhunting equipment, including bow sights.
1937	Michigan holds nation's first archery deer season.
1940	The interchangeable arrow point is introduced.
Early 1940s	The first glass-limbed bow is introduced.
1943	Commercially-produced bow quivers are marketed.
1946	Doug Easton introduces the aluminum arrow.
1950	Max Hamilton produces plastic vanes.
1951	Fred Bear develops unidirectional fiberglass for use on bow limbs.
1951	Dacron bowstring is introduced.
Early 1950s	Groves and American separately introduce two of the first commercially-made overdraws.
1953	First arrow rest is introduced.
1957	First replaceable-blade broadhead is marketed.
1961	Pope and Young Club is formed to bolster bowhunting image.
1960s	Hollis Allen introduces and patents the compound bow.
1968	Archery Manufacturers Organization standards are approved.
1973	Gordon Plastics produce carbon glass arrow shafts.
1974	Mel Stanislawski introduces the launcher-type arrow rest.
1978	Jennings develops the cable guard.
1981	Gordon Plastics introduces graphite and fiberglass arrow shafts.
1983	PSE announces production of the cam bow.
1987	AFC introduces all-carbon arrow shafts.
1988	Fred Bear dies.
1990	Chuck Adams completes bowhunting's first North American Super Slam in taking all 27 recognized big-game animals.

completed the coveted Grand Slam on wild sheep.''

Burke, of course, was talking about Chuck Adams, the most successful bowhunter of all time. Chuck is also a prolific writer, with more than 2,000 magazine stories and seven books about bowhunting. For many modern bowhunters, he is already (or is fast becoming) the next ''archer-emeritus and the patron saint of bowhunting.''

The Milestones Of Modern Bowhunting

You have been exposed to some of the great modern bowhunters in order to help you understand the modern history of bowhunting. There have been inventions and accomplishments which have shaped our bowhunting history. Bowhunters have moved from yew wood bows to bows with glass limbs and machined aluminum risers, and from hand-carved arrows to super-straight and lightweight aluminum and space-age carbon.

Bear, in *The Archer's Bible*, summed up the history of bowhunting: ''After the perfection of weapons for the use of gunpowder made the bow all but obsolete for warfare, it still retained its popularity in many parts of the world as a sporting and hunting arm.''

3

Understanding Compound Bows

Ambient temperature is 10 degrees below zero, but it doesn't matter. An 8-point whitetail is 70 yards away. Provided I keep quiet, the buck should pass within 20 yards of my tree stand as he sneaks through the snow-covered valley. Despite the bitter cold that has me bundled up like the Stay-Puff Marshmallow Man, he wears the same coat he did last summer, only it's thicker. He is the 11th deer I have seen today.

The other 10 were does. Given these conditions, and the opportunity, I would have taken one, but they all plodded past my stand without stopping on the way to the open field. One eventually came so close I could have jumped on her back. As she came toward me, I drew back and waited for her to stop. My 20-yard pin followed her down the trail until she was right under my tree stand, but she kept going.

My stand is in a tree that cracks and splits. The sound comes from the sap inside freezing and expanding until it breaks open the tree's veins. That sound makes me wonder what would happen if my blood began to freeze. It's then that I want to stomp my feet.

Suddenly, the buck walks out from behind a clump of trees. I pull back on the bowstring slightly, prompting my arm and back muscles to tighten. They are stiff, perhaps numb from the cold. I hold the abbreviated draw for a fraction of a second, then let down and feel blood rushing into the muscles.

He walks out from behind the tree, head down, smelling the snow. He is not suspicious. I breathe deep and remind myself to stay calm and release clean. I am suddenly very warm.

About 40 yards away he walks behind another tree. It is time to draw. I hope for one fluid motion, but my muscles sputter and I must grit my teeth to reach full draw. As he walks into the open, I settle into my anchor, nudge the kisser button into the familiar feel of the corner of my mouth and peer through the peep sight. I put the top pin behind his front shoulder.

During the next 15 seconds he walks quietly and slowly down the trail. It seems like a full minute, but I am comfortably staying at full draw, waiting for my shot. He stops 20 yards away, broadside. I concentrate on one aiming point, then release.

The arrow's red fletch intersects my aiming point and I hear the arrow's coursing punch and see the deer jump. Two quick bounds, then he stops. Thirty yards away he turns and looks back at the place where he stood just seconds ago. Seemingly unconcerned, he turns and trots another 40 yards, then suddenly he stumbles and falls. The arrow had done its job.

Despite the bitter cold that freezes sap and cracks wood, my modern compound performed flawlessly. Even with stiff, unstretched muscles I was able to hold the bow at full draw for an extended length of time. And despite traveling 20 yards and hitting ribs on both sides of the chest cavity, the broadhead-tipped shaft went through the buck and into the ground. A lot of the credit for this successful hunt should go to my compound bow.

Without 65 percent let-off at full draw, I would not have made the shot. I could not have held the 70-pound draw for that length of time with a recurve. And I could not have drawn the recurve until the deer went behind the tree. If I had been using anything other than a compound, I would not have taken that deer.

Let's compare a 70-pound, draw-weight recurve and a 70-pound, draw-weight compound. As you draw back the bowstring on a recurve, draw weight increases until full draw is reached. At that point, you've reached peak weight. With a compound, peak draw weight is reached sooner, and there is a let-off of 50 or 65 percent from the peak draw weight before you reach full draw. In addition to reduced holding weight, there's another significant advantage: With both bows at full draw, the compound stores more energy than the recurve because more energy was expended in order to bring the compound to full draw, even though it doesn't feel like it. This energy is the source of the faster arrow speed and greater kinetic energy produced by a mod-

Compound bows provide faster arrow speeds by imparting more energy into the arrow's flight. The more kinetic energy, the greater the penetration potential. Its let-off also allows a bowhunter to remain at full draw longer.

The author (center) accepts congratulations from his guide on taking a P&Y record prong-horn that came into the decoy. The author used a bow with a mild cam, a cross between a round wheel and a cam.

ern compound bow which results in clean kills.

Understanding Wheels And Cams

Various wheels and cams are available on modern compound bows. When looking at these eccentrics, remember that round wheels are smoother and slower than cams. Cams are not magical power boosters. If you want 5 percent more energy, a cam will give it to you; however, you will need to exert 5 percent more energy as you draw the bow. Now, here's a look at the basic designs of both compound wheels and cams.

Round Wheels. Round wheels have a smooth draw. Often preferred by finger shooters, they are more forgiving than cams. When a round wheel is drawn, the draw weight steadily increases until peak draw weight is reached, then it gradually decreases until full draw. Round wheels are smoother and quieter than cams; however, they also store less energy, producing slower arrow speeds.

Mild Cams. A cross between a round wheel and a cam is called a mild cam. Different manufacturers use different names for this middle-of-the-road eccentric. Mild cams combine the round wheel's smooth draw, quiet release and forgiving nature with the cam's faster arrow speed and flatter trajectory. However, they are not as smooth as a round wheel or as fast as a cam; they are somewhere between the two.

Cams. Egg-shaped cams, which were introduced in the early 1980s, store more energy. Therefore, they deliver between 5 and 15 percent more arrow speed than the normal round wheel. That increased arrow speed results in a flatter trajectory which can be more forgiving when range estimation errors occur. A cam-operated bow reaches peak draw weight sooner than a round wheel or mild cam; however, it must be drawn at that high peak weight over a greater distance. Plus, a cam-operated bow has a more abrupt let-off. It is not as smooth as the round wheel or mild cam. Cams do not forgive release errors as easily and are most often shot by archers using release aids. Cams can also cause more game-spooking noise.

Whether you select cams or wheels depends upon your hunting situation and preferred hunting style. When short-range, tree-stand hunting, shots are usually taken at less than 20 yards. A quiet, smooth-drawing round wheel or mild cam might be the best option in this

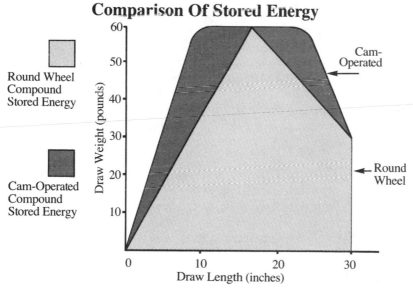

This force-draw curve illustrates the difference in stored energy generated by a round-wheel compound bow versus that produced by a cam-operated compound. Round wheels do provide a smoother motion, however.

situation. When in a tree stand, you shoot at the shorter, known distances so a super-flat trajectory will not be as important.

If you need to quickly estimate rather than precisely measure distances when hunting, a cam may be the best choice. This situation occurs when hunting near open fields, in the West or with the still-hunting method. Under these conditions, a cam shoots a flatter-flying arrow.

Super fast bows were popular in the late 1980s and early 1990s; however, the smoother, quieter mild cam is beginning to surpass fast bows. A mild cam is a good compromise. Many manufacturers already have mild cams available—some offer two eccentrics ranging between a round wheel and a cam.

Hoyt, for example, in addition to having round-wheel and speed-cam bows, offers an energy wheel and a soft cam on the Super Slam bow. The energy wheel, a round wheel with a cam-shaped oval lobe on one side, is about 5 percent faster than the round wheel. This lobe provides increased draw weight like the round wheel until it flattens off on top, dropping off more sharply near full draw. More energy is expended to bring the bow to full draw resulting in more stored energy. The soft cam is about 5 percent faster than the energy wheel. The force-draw curve with the soft cam is steeper on both sides with a longer distance at peak weight. And, with a speed cam, the sides of the force-draw curve are even steeper. The speed cam is about 5 percent faster than the soft cam.

Understanding Handle Design

Three basic handle designs are featured on compound bows: deflexed, reflexed and I-beam. The type of riser will, in part, determine arrow speed and arrow flight. However, as with eccentrics, you can't have everything. Riser designs producing faster arrow speeds are less forgiving; greater care must be taken in order to assure a proper release.

Deflexed Riser. A deflexed riser "bows out" from the shooter. It forms a "v" from the riser's center to the shooter. When using a deflexed riser, your bow hand will be farther from your body than the bow's top or bottom. This design's advantage is that it is less affected by a less-than-clean release. Even though it is more forgiving, however, it produces a slower arrow than the other two designs because of the shorter power stroke. (Power stroke is the distance during which the arrow is actually propelled by the bowstring.)

Reflexed Riser. A reflexed riser actually bends toward the shooter and away from the limb pockets. This increases the power stroke and,

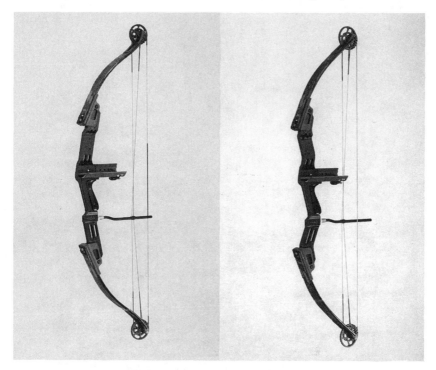

A deflexed riser (left) is the most forgiving but also the slowest while the reflexed (right) is the fastest but also requires a proper release. The I-beam riser falls in between the deflexed and reflexed on both counts.

subsequently, arrow speed. Although a reflexed riser is the fastest, it also is the most finicky about a clean release.

I-Beam Riser. An I-beam riser fits in a nitch between slower deflexed risers and faster reflexed risers. An I-beam riser is straight up and down. The place where the bow hand grips the riser is typically in line with the limb pockets. And like mild cams, the I-beam produces moderately fast arrow speeds (like a reflexed handle) but is moderately forgiving (like a deflexed handle).

The never-ending problem with bowhunting is that you can't have everything. A deflexed riser is more accurate, but slower. A reflexed riser is faster, but less forgiving. And once again, there is a middle-of-the-road option: the I-beam riser.

The handle design you choose depends upon your hunting situation and preferred hunting technique. Beginning bowhunters should select a deflexed riser; more experienced shooters, especially if using a release aid, may prefer a faster, reflexed-riser design.

Finger shooters generally will need a compound with greater axle-to-axle length in order to avoid finger pinch. This archer is using a finger tab with a built-in spacer to help avoid the pinch.

Understanding Axle-To-Axle Measurement

The axle-to-axle measurement is the distance from the axle of one eccentric to the axle of the other. This distance has been shortened as bowhunters search for more arrow speed. Shortening the axle-to-axle length increases the bow's speed. Some bows have extremely short axle-to-axle lengths and radical eccentrics, while others have longer axle-to-axle lengths and more rounded eccentrics.

"You can't have everything in a bow design," says Chuck Adams. "The shorter a bow is axle-to-axle, all else being equal, the more energy it stores at full draw and the faster it is. This is because the shorter you go axle-to-axle on a bow, the bigger your wheels or cams have to be to give you your proper draw length. That's a mechanical fact. The larger those wheels or cams are, the more energy they store. So a 40- or 41-inch bow always has larger diameter wheels or cams at your draw length than a 46- or 48-inch bow. Therefore, the shorter bow with the necessary wheels or cams is faster and stores more energy."

"On the flip side," Chuck continues, "if you are a finger shooter, you are not going to shoot as accurately with a shorter axle-to-axle-length bow because the string angle around your finger is considerably sharper and you experience what is called 'finger pinch.' If you go to the biggest national archery tournament, you'll see that finger shooters almost invariably are shooting bows that are at least 45 inches long or longer, because they get a much crisper string release. There's not as much binding up on the fingers because of the bowstring angle. If you're a finger shooter, you're forced to shoot a little longer axle-to-axle-length compound than if you're a release-aid shooter. A release aid grips the string at one point and is not prone to binding so you can shoot those short, 40- to 41-inch, axle-to-axle-length bows and enjoy extra speed and energy."

Dwight Schuh says he prefers a 43- to 45-inch, axle-to-axle-length bow primarily because it offers a little more stability. "Years ago all the compound bows were 48 inches long," he says. "Now 46 inches is a long one and standard is probably 42 or 43. Even with a release, I guess I prefer bows that are 43 to 45 inches long, because I feel like there's a little more stability just by virtue of the length of the bow. I don't like using a stabilizer because I don't like to pack around the added weight. I feel that a little bit longer bow gives you a little more proportional stability."

Understanding Bowstrings

Modern compound bows have either Fast-Flight or Dacron bow-

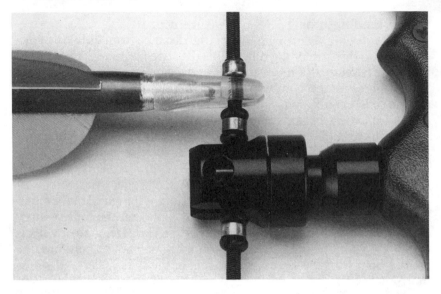

Bowhunters who use a release aid don't have to worry about finger pinch so they can shoot bows with shorter axle-to-axle distances. As shown here, the release grips the string in only one spot.

strings. Dacron, which was the industry standard for many years, has the tendency to stretch over time. Some of the more affordable, entry-level bows are manufactured with Dacron strings. Fast-Flight strings do not stretch. Also, Fast-Flight strings are lighter than Dacron. Just as a lighter arrow will travel faster than a heavier arrow, a lighter Fast-Flight string will travel faster than a heavier Dacron string. This faster-moving string propels the arrow shaft faster. A Fast-Flight string results in a net increase in arrow speed by 3 to 12 feet per second, according to Bob Ragsdale, an engineer at Precision Shooting Equipment. "A string on a compound bow that does not stretch, contract-stretch and then contract again during a single shot cycle can truly add 3 to 12 fps to your present arrow with your bow on the same peak-holding weight," he says. "Not an asset that should be poo-pooed too quickly."

Understanding Bow Limbs

Bow limbs, either straight or recurve, are constructed of various materials. Straight bow limbs do not have the reverse curve of a recurve. Instead, they continue along a curve from the limb pockets to the tips. Near the end of the recurve limbs, however, the curve reverses away from the shooter.

Bow limbs are made from fiberglass, foam, wood and carbon. Wood-core limbs may have a tendency to crush over time. This reduces draw weight and may require retuning. Limbs made of fiberglass, fiberglass and foam, and fiberglass and carbon are impervious to the elements and will not crush.

Understanding Let-Off

Most modern compound bows have a let-off of 50 or 65 percent. These let-offs allow the bowhunter to hold only a fraction of the bow's peak draw weight at full draw. A compound with a 50 percent let-off and 60-pound draw weight requires a holding weight of only 30 pounds. A compound with a 65 percent let-off and 60-pound draw weight requires a holding weight of 26 pounds. With a lower holding weight, the bowhunter can stay at full draw longer and more comfortably, waiting for the best shot opportunity.

Understanding Kinetic Energy

When the bowstring is released, the arrow propels toward the target. That arrow, based on its velocity and weight, possesses kinetic energy. Kinetic energy is the force with which an arrow strikes its target. The more kinetic energy the arrow has, the greater the penetration potential. "Penetration is directly related to kinetic energy," says Norb Mullaney, professional engineer and director of bow testing for a bowhunting publication, "We have established beyond a shadow of a doubt the relationship between kinetic energy and penetration."

The projectile's weight affects penetration. Assuming velocity is equal, place the points of two nails on a pine board, tap the nails in just far enough so they stand up. Take a 20-ounce carpenter's hammer in one hand and a 4-ounce upholster's hammer in the other. Bring both hammers up, then down at the same speed onto the nail heads. Repeat this, bringing them down at the same speed. The heavier hammer pounds a nail farther into the board than the lighter hammer, all things being equal. The heavier the object set in motion, the greater its penetration potential.

Assuming the projectile's weight remains the same, the object's speed affects penetration. Place the points of two nails into the pine board. Take a 20-ounce carpenter's hammer in each hand. With one hammer, strike the nail with a quick blow. Bring the other hammer down more slowly onto the nail's head. The fast-traveling hammer pounds the nail in farther than the slow hammer. The faster the object travels, the greater its penetration potential.

To penetrate deer-sized animals, the minimum acceptable kinetic energy is 40 foot-pounds; 45 to 50 foot-pounds is preferred. For game weighing more than 500 pounds, such as elk, moose or bear, the minimum acceptable kinetic energy is 50 foot-pounds; 55 to 65 foot-pounds is preferred.

You can obtain the information needed to calculate the kinetic energy of your hunting bow by visiting your local archery pro shop. First, determine your arrow shaft's speed by shooting it through the shop's chronograph. Your arrow speed, or velocity (V) will be shown in feet per second. Next, weigh your hunting arrow, including broadhead, to determine your total arrow weight (W). The pro shop should have a reloader's scale for this purpose. Plug these two numbers (V and W) into the following formula. The answer will be in foot-pounds.

$$\frac{\text{Velocity x Velocity x Weight}}{450,240} = \text{Kinetic Energy}$$

If your kinetic energy is above the recommended minimums mentioned above, terrific. If not, visit your local archery dealer and follow his suggestions for boosting your bow's kinetic energy. Or study Chapter 11, "Tips For Increasing Arrow Velocity." Increasing arrow velocity will increase your bow's kinetic energy.

4

Selecting The Best Bow

Selecting a bow that fits you, your hunting needs and your pock-
etbook can be fairly easy. The difficulty is that there may be many
bows on the rack that would most likely fit you and your hunting
style. If you bought any one of them and spent enough time tuning it,
chances are you could get the bow to shoot well. To further complicate the selection process, many of the bowhunters who frequent archery pro shops have their own favorite bow brand. Sure, it shoots
well for them, but it may not be the right bow for you.

The purpose here is to present the practical know-how and information necessary so you can make an informed and educated selection. This chapter introduces the novice to the bow selection process;
however, it also contains valuable information for hunters with vary-
ing skills and knowledge. If you already have a bow, this is an opportunity to determine whether the bow fits you well and meets your
bowhunting needs.

First, you must decide which game animal you want to bowhunt.
Perhaps you want a bow for hunting white-tailed deer. Or maybe you
want a bow to shoot for recreation and eventually work into hunting
big game. Perhaps you want to upgrade your equipment and purchase
a bow that takes larger, big-game animals, such as elk and moose.
Take some time to figure out what you want in a bow, and what you
would like to hunt. Then head for your local pro shop. A good archery
shop will be able to fill your needs.

Determine Draw Length

The first thing you need to know is your draw length. Draw length can be determined two ways. To determine it at home, stand up straight and place the end of a yardstick against the center of your chest (perpendicular to your body). Keeping the stick parallel to the floor, extend both arms forward as far as possible, bringing your hands together flat on the yardstick. The distance to the ends of your fingers is your approximate draw length.

The easiest and most accurate method to determine draw length, however, is to let your local archery pro shop operator do it. Most pro shop staffs use a long arrow shaft that is marked in 1-inch increments which you actually draw back in a bow. Once you are properly anchored at full draw, the staff person checks the inch-marking on the arrow just beyond the front edge of the handle to determine proper draw length.

These are the two most common methods to determine draw length. However, be forewarned that your draw length can change if you change your hunting stance. Although the accepted stance for target archery is closed (both feet parallel to the face of the target) most bowhunters shoot with a slightly open stance (both feet turned slightly toward the target). The more you turn toward the target, the shorter your draw length. (Proper stance and shooting form are discussed in Chapter 13, "Proven Practice Techniques.")

Determine Preferred Draw Weight

Most modern compound bows can be adjusted over a 15-pound draw weight range, normally from 35 to 50, 45 to 60, 55 to 70 or 65 to 80 pounds. Peak draw weight can be adjusted. Turning both limb bolts the same number of turns clockwise increases draw weight; turning counterclockwise decreases draw weight.

If you are selecting your first bow, choose one with a draw weight you can handle comfortably. Moderate-weight bows will seem difficult to draw at first because you're using new muscles. But, with practice, you can develop the ability to draw back heavier bows. Because most manufacturers' draw-weight ranges overlap, you can select the 55- to 70-pound draw-weight range if your comfortable draw weight is 60 pounds and still increase the draw weight up to 10 pounds as your muscles become stronger. In this case, choosing a 45- to 60-pound, draw-weight bow will limit your long-term use and enjoyment of this bow.

Some states have minimum draw-weight or draw-length requirements for hunting. Be sure to check your state game and fish depart-

An easy way to determine your draw length is with a yardstick. Press the front end against your upper chest near the throat and slide your hands, fingers extended, out till your arms are fully extended. Where the fingertips touch is your draw length.

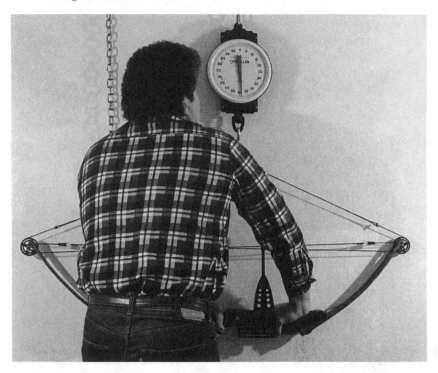

Most archery pro shops will have a scale rigged up so you can accurately determine your bow's peak draw weight and the holding weight. Most bows have a 15-pound adjustable weight range.

ment's hunting regulations before making your final selection.

Select A Bow That Fits You

Walk into any archery pro shop or page through any mail-order catalog and you probably will be overwhelmed by the smorgasbord of bows available. Some have wheels, others have cams. There will be terms and claims that you probably don't understand. That's why first-time bow buyers are better served by going to an archery pro shop. Archery pro shops have professionals who lead you through the bow selection process and find two or three makes and models that will most likely fit you. They also show you some basic techniques on shooting form, anchor point and release.

How do you know if a bow fits you well? Shoot it. It is difficult, if not impossible, to determine whether a bow shoots well in your hands by standing in a store and drawing it back and letting it down. Most pro shops have shooting lanes where you can shoot with different models before making your choice of a new bow.

Tell the archery pro staffer what you hope to hunt. Then follow his advice. Most modern compounds produce the required energy to harvest deer-sized game. However, if you want to hunt larger game, such as elk or moose, be sure the bow can generate the kinetic energy that's required to stop an animal of that size.

Many top-quality bows are available. Sometimes, the decision to select one above all the others will probably depend upon which bow "feels" best in your hands. Trust your gut feeling—provided the better feeling bow shoots as accurately as the other top bow.

Upgrade To A Better Bow

At some point you will want a better bow. Today's hunting bows can basically be divided into three classes: smooth bows, moderately-smooth/moderately-fast bows and fast bows.

Fast bows shoot faster speed arrows with flatter trajectory. With that flatter trajectory, range-estimation errors are less of a problem. This can be especially beneficial if you hunt areas where it's difficult to determine the distance to the target or where shots will be taken at longer ranges. A fast arrow possesses more kinetic energy than a slower arrow of the same weight.

However, there are disadvantages with faster bows. Generally, faster bows can produce more game-spooking noise during the release, and are typically less forgiving.

Smooth bows, meanwhile, are quieter to shoot, more comfortable to draw through the peak weight and smoother to release. They also are more forgiving.

However, there are disadvantages, too. A slower-flying arrow has less kinetic energy, and a greater trajectory than a fast, flatter-flying arrow. If hunting from a tree stand where shots are generally at close range and distances along shooting lanes are already determined, you'll find these smooth, quiet bows to be a boon. If shooting a smooth bow at longer distances, determine the distance as accurately as possible before you shoot.

A leading whitetail authority and consultant to a major bow manufacturer, Myles Keller says he looks for a shootable bow that is extremely quiet. "The most important quality is that the bow has to be functionally quiet not only when you release an arrow but when you draw," he says. "I want a quiet bow."

Wayne Carlton, a member of the Bear Archery Pro Staff, says, "When I look for a bow, I want one that shoots flat, not just because I like speed, but because I like the forgiveness it gives me if I do not

The next step is to select a bow within your draw length and draw weight range that feels best to you. If at all possible, shoot the bow before you buy it. Most archery pro shops have a range where this can be done.

A quick way of increasing bow speed is to simply switch to using carbon arrows which are lighter than aluminum arrows and have a smaller diameter. This means they will fly faster, all else being equal.

accurately determine whether the animal is 30 or 35 yards away.'' Carlton shoots an 85-pound draw-weight bow with 65 percent let-off. ''At this weight I don't have to worry about multiple pins,'' he says. ''I shoot it like I would a BB gun. I shoot one pin and lock it in position when I'm hunting on the ground at 30 yards. If I am hunting in a tree stand, I'll lock it in at 20 yards.

''I can sight my bow in for 30 yards,'' Carlton continues, ''and at 40 yards it is 4½ inches low. At 20 yards, it is 2 inches high. At 10 yards it is just about an inch low. I know that from shooting a lot of arrows and using a 1-inch graph to find out where it is shooting.''

Bowhunting legend Chuck Adams says accuracy is the most important factor, and that speed and quietness are also important. ''These three factors tend to work against one another in a bow,'' he says. ''You get a quiet bow that is accurate but isn't very fast. Or you can get a fast bow, but it might not be very quiet or it might be marginally accurate. Accuracy is the most important consideration for me. The Hoyt Super Slam is the only bow that combines those three for me. For example, my Super Slam bow, set at 72½ pounds, shoots a 608-grain, 2219 arrow at 210 fps. My Pro Vantage bow, which is longer axle-to-axle (48 inches instead of 43), shoots the very same arrow (a 608-grain 2219) at the same speed, set at 85 pounds of draw weight. By going to the Super Slam, I am getting the same speed, while dropping 12½ pounds off the bow's peak weight. It's that much faster. The Super Slam riser is almost I-beamed, so it's a good compromise between accuracy and performance.''

Judd Cooney who shoots an Oregon bow says, ''I shoot at 90 pounds for everything. I want to shoot the same bow and the same arrow weight all the time. I experiment around until I get something to work, then I stay with it. And I don't change. Keep it simple.''

5

Selecting The Best Arrow

Bowhunters can do everything else right, but if they shoot the wrong arrow shafts, their setups won't shoot like they should. Selecting the right arrow requires knowing your peak draw weight, hunting arrow length and arrow-point weight. That's it. Peak draw weight already has been covered. Hunting arrow length is simply your draw length plus an inch for broadhead clearance. If your draw length is 29 inches, your arrow should be 30 inches. Arrow point weight is the weight of your field point or broadhead (which should be the same). With these three numbers and an arrow shaft selection chart, you can select the right arrow shaft. It's that simple.

A properly spined arrow is one that has the right shaft stiffness. When you release the bowstring, the bow's energy is transferred to the arrow shaft. Shafts typically flex, or oscillate, when they are first propelled. A properly spined arrow recovers and flies true.

Selecting the correct aluminum and carbon shafts will be covered in the first half of this chapter. In the second half, the two different views regarding arrow weight will be examined. One view leans toward a heavier shaft for a quieter bow and greater kinetic energy; while the other prefers a lighter shaft for a flatter trajectory that is more forgiving of range-estimation errors.

Selecting An Aluminum Hunting Arrow

First introduced in 1946 by Doug Easton, aluminum hunting

shafts are preferred by most bowhunters. Aluminum shafts are consistent, accurate and effective. Today you can purchase aluminum shafts that are straight within a tolerance of $^{15}/_{1000}$ of an inch.

In selecting an aluminum hunting arrow, find your hunting-arrow length (draw length plus one inch) on the horizontal axis of the Easton shaft-selection chart on pages 240 and 241. Then, find your peak draw weight under the correct arrow-point weight and eccentric on the vertical axis. Follow the hunting-arrow-length column down and the peak draw-weight over to the right. At the intersection will be the arrow shafts properly spined for your setup. That point of intersection also identifies the shaft model and shaft weight. (Easton's *A Guide to Bowhunting With Easton Arrow Shafts* is available by sending $1 to Easton Aluminum, A Guide To Bowhunting With Easton Arrow Shafts, 5040 W. Harold Gatty Dr., Salt Lake City, UT 84116-2897.)

Selecting The Right Carbon Hunting Arrow

It wasn't that long ago that carbon arrows were used primarily by field archery competitors and a few bowhunters. But, as more hunters were exposed to and experimented with carbon shafts, an increasing ing number of shooters began selecting carbon arrows made by AFC, Beman or Easton to fill their hunting needs. Today, you'll find at least one bowhunter in camp who shoots—and swears by—carbon shafts.

Chatfield, Minnesota-based AFC first introduced carbon arrow shafts in 1987. What had been an uphill battle as the company entered a market dominated by aluminum arrows has resulted in AFC securing a niche in the hunting arrow market.

In 1989, a French company, Beman Archery, introduced its own carbon arrow shaft which over time has also secured some market share. Easton, the world's largest aluminum arrow maker, has responded by producing a pultruded carbon arrow shaft of its own.

Carbon shafts first gained attention in international archery competitions, where they were the arrow of choice of a number of world and Olympic champions. Properly spined carbon shafts are lighter than aluminum which means they are faster, have a flatter trajectory and are more durable. These were major pluses for the target shooters, and bowhunters searching for more speed and flatter trajectory gradually have been attracted to the slender carbon shafts. Now carbon arrows are also available in camo designs.

There are two ways in which you can select the correct carbon shaft for your setup. If you are using a properly spined aluminum arrow for your setup, you can select a corresponding properly spined carbon shaft in one quick step from AFC and Beman comparison/

Whether you choose an aluminum arrow or a carbon arrow to propel your broadhead, you'll have a potent combination. This bow is equipped with a 2-inch overdraw to reduce arrow length and increase arrow speed.

conversion charts found on Page 242 of the Appendix. (Easton has a conversion chart, too.) Or, by using your calculated peak bow weight and your correct hunting arrow length, you can select the correct carbon shaft from shaft selection charts provided by the carbon arrow makers.

To use the Beman shaft-selection chart, for example, determine your correct hunting arrow length and your calculated peak bow weight. Hunting-arrow length, of course, is simply draw length plus one inch. To determine calculated peak draw weight, measure your bow's peak draw weight. Then use Beman's bow weight system to determine the calculated bow weight. Using the arrow length and calculated weight, you can easily choose the properly spined carbon arrow from the Beman chart.

Fletch: Feathers Or Vanes?

Whether your fletch is made of feathers or vanes, it must control arrow flight and keep the broadhead from planing. Under ideal conditions, both feathers and vanes are capable of doing just that. However, plastic vanes have an advantage over feathers when used in wet conditions. Even with an application of waterproofing liquid, feathered fletch can still get wet. Because wet feathers weigh more than dry feathers, arrow flight could easily be influenced. Also, wet feathers often are matted, affecting the feathers' ability to control the broadhead.

Arrow-Weight Debate

Generally, these are the views on arrow weight: Heavier arrows make for a quieter bow and more kinetic energy; lighter arrows are faster, providing a flatter trajectory which is more forgiving of range estimation errors.

"What you need to do is find the arrow that gives you the best accuracy with a given bow," says Dwight Schuh. "And I think a lightweight arrow is going to give you a little bit more leeway in terms of range estimation and vertical accuracy. It's not that I favor a superlight arrow; I favor getting the most out of a particular tackle. I would be stupid to shoot 2219s off a 55-pound bow. Even though they may be spined correctly for it, I'd get lousy trajectory with that. So I drop down 150 to 200 grains and still get good trajectory and I get adequate penetration on animals up to the size of elk."

Dwight shoots a 55-pound, draw-weight bow with energy wheels. His draw length is 31 inches, but he shoots with a 5-inch overdraw. He is able to shorten arrow length to 27 inches and shoots 27-inch 2213s for elk.

Even though some hunters have switched to carbon arrow shafts, Chuck Adams uses only aluminum arrow shafts. Adams prefers medium to heavy arrows for a quieter shot and better arrow flight.

"To put this into a nutshell," he says, "I think a person should stick with the AMO (Archery Manufacturers' Organization) recommendations of 6 grains of arrow weight per pound of draw weight. I think that's a conservative minimum—not an extreme minimum at all. So with a 60-pound draw weight, you can shoot a 360-grain arrow. Some people would say that's way too light for elk. Well, I don't think so. I think it's a reasonably good minimum. The 60 pounds of draw weight has a lot more to do with how much energy that bow produces than the arrow weight does. Sure the arrow weight is part of the equation, but I think if you stick with that 6-grain minimum, you're in a safe limit. If your arrows are not producing enough kinetic energy to kill the animal, the problem is insufficient draw weight —not light arrows.

"Of course, this assumes structural strength is equal," Dwight continues. "If you shoot a real light arrow and a flimsy broadhead just to get your arrow weight down, the thing might come apart when it hits an elk. Whereas if you are shooting a big, heavy arrow with a big, solid broadhead, it probably won't come apart. (This assumes arrow strength is the same.)

"The difference between Chuck Adams and me is not so much that he favors heavy arrows and I favor light arrows," says Schuh. "It's that he shoots an 80-pound bow and I shoot a 55-pound bow. There's a major difference right there. I obviously am going to shoot a lot lighter arrows because I'm shooting a lot lower draw weight. If you figure out the grain weight per pound of draw weight, my arrows are not that much different than his."

NAHC Bowhunting Advisory Council member Judd Cooney shoots Beman carbon arrow shafts. "I think it's pretty academic," he says. "If you make a good shot, you kill an animal. There's only one phase of death—and that's dead. Most bows and most arrows on the market will do that, if you put the arrow in the right place. I think it's not so much the equipment, as it is the hunter who is behind the equipment.

"I like an arrow that is heavy enough, that will penetrate and that will fly very flat," Cooney continues. "I use a heavy draw-weight bow and I use a heavy arrow so I've got the best of both worlds. I have seen more problems with ultra-light shafts because under ideal situations they work fine. However, as soon as you release, it is no longer an ideal situation. So I want an arrow that will do its job under the most difficult circumstances. I feel that a heavy arrow with a flat trajectory and good velocity is what you want. Unfortunately, the only way you can get that is to shoot a heavier bow."

Judd shoots a bow with a 90-pound draw weight and 32-inch arrow shafts. Using 32-inch 2317 aluminum shafts, he says he gets an arrow velocity of 217 fps. With 80/100 carbon shafts, he gets an arrow speed of 237 fps.

"I think I am getting better penetration with a carbon shaft," says Cooney, who shot through an elk at 35 yards using the 80/100's. "I hit a rib going in and a rib going out. The arrow went completely through the elk and was about 45 yards on the other side of him. Now I've never had that happen before—I'm used to looking 10 or 15 yards on the other side.

"I took a shot at a buck last year that I would not have taken if I was not shooting the carbon shafts I was shooting," he says. "I grunted a buck in and he quartered to me—he came in with his shoulder right to me. I shot him right through the point of the shoulder. I shattered his front shoulder, and the arrow went through, burying the broadhead in the femur. The whole shaft was inside the deer undam-

Beman, one of three major carbon arrow shaft makers, puts out a full line of carbon arrow shafts. They also put out an arrow shaft conversion table which you can find in this book's Appendix.

aged. I would not have taken that shot with an aluminum shaft.

"I took another big whitetail in Canada last fall," Cooney continues. "I shot him at 35 yards. The arrow went through in back of the shoulder on the on-side, then it went completely through and shattered the shoulder on the off-side. The arrow was hanging out by the tip of the fletching. I got some fantastic penetration. The thing about that is, I don't know if I would have gotten the same penetration with an aluminum shaft. I don't think I would have, but that's just an opinion. It comes down to a gut feeling. I think I'm getting far better penetration on game animals with a carbon shaft than I would with aluminum."

One possibility, Cooney says, is that a carbon arrow's narrow shaft means that all the energy is being driven down a narrow projectile. "It does not buckle like an aluminum shaft," he says. "If you've ever seen slow-motion photography of an aluminum shaft hitting a target, it will bend over. A carbon shaft won't do that. I think that energy is going in a much narrower, straighter line, and you get better penetration."

Cooney says he does not think the arrow shaft's friction has much to do with it—carbon shafts are smaller in diameter than aluminum shafts. "When that goes through the flesh, I don't care what it cuts," he says. "The flesh, fat, hair and hide are very flexible and fall in right behind it, grabbing the shaft and everything else, unlike ethafoam (used in commercial targets). I think it's that driving force. I also think that, engineering-wise, somebody could prove that on the impact.

"If you take an aluminum shaft and shoot at, say, a half-inch piece of plywood," Cooney continues, "you'll wreck the shaft. It will shatter the shaft or break it. The carbon shaft will go right through it like a bullet. I think it is because of the shaft's small diameter, the tremendous driving force and the thick walls."

Chuck Adams, who prefers aluminum, says: "I'm not sure I belong to either school of thought, to be honest. But I lean toward medium- to heavyweight shafts for animals over 300 pounds. That would be from black bear-sized animals up through caribou and elk and similar-sized animals. I shoot the medium- to heavyweight shafts because my bow is quieter. There is less vibration through my bow which means my bow is less likely to malfunction with limb breakage or handle breakage or cable failure due to vibration. I get a little better accuracy with medium- to heavyweight shafts because they are not flying quite as fast. So the bigger animals, those 300 pounds and larger, I want to shoot with a full-sized broadhead, preferably a 4-blade broadhead for maximum tissue damage. I just can't see pushing an arrow above 220 or 230 fps with a broadhead that big because accuracy problems almost always result.

"For smaller animals, deer-sized animals on down, I prefer a medium- to lightweight shaft," Adams continues. "SuperLite aluminum shafts, which are defined as any aluminum shaft with a wall thickness of $14/1000$ of an inch or less, are my preference wherever deer-sized and smaller animals are in open country. With a SuperLite shaft, I get an average of 15 fps more with my bow. I'm not so worried about shooting a big broadhead on animals the size of deer and smaller, so I go down in broadhead size, maybe from four to three blades, or from $1\frac{3}{8}$- or $1\frac{1}{2}$-inch broadhead to a broadhead slightly over 1 inch in diameter. I get the extra speed for flatter trajectory in more open country where shots are likely to be longer and range estimation might be a faster and less deliberate process.

"For big animals like moose and brown bear," he says, "I normally shoot an arrow that's over 600 grains, not a lot over. For example, on my big Alaskan brown bear, I shot it with a 604-grain arrow. I normally shoot a broadhead in the 150- to 160-grain range with that weight arrow."

According to Adams, the most hotly debated issue regarding

For taking an animal of this size, experts like Chuck Adams advise bowhunters to use the heaviest tackle they can. He says a heavy arrow results in less bow vibration and greater accuracy.

The author chose a 70-pound PSE Fire-Flite bow for taking this 285-pound black bear in Canada. The bear scored 18¹/₁₆ points, good enough for entry in the Pope and Young record book.

light versus heavy arrows is not even debatable. "It's cut and dried and it has to do with penetration," he says. "I have numerous arrow penetration tests with different shafts out of the same bows. For example, one test started with a 60-pound bow. I shot arrows, properly spined for that bow, from about 600 grains down to 375 grains. I conducted my penetration tests with broadheads in a vegetable-tanned leather baffling system I designed that closely approximates an animal's body. I've shot through dead animals quite a bit and this baffling system gives me almost identical results, except it's more precise because I don't have ribs or soft spots in the body to contend with. Every layer that I shoot through has been shaved to a particular thickness at a tannery so it's a very precise way to do it.

"On paper, " Adams continues, "for every 100 grains of arrow weight that you take off on average, you lose 2½ to 3 percent of your kinetic energy in the shaft at one yard in front of the bow. For example, if a 60-pound bow with a 600-grain arrow gets 50 foot-pounds of kinetic energy, a 500-grain arrow would only lose about 1.5 foot pounds of kinetic energy. That is not worth talking about in my estimation. Even if you drop from a 600- to a 400-grain arrow, you're only dropping in front of the bow one yard about 5 or 6 percent. And if you start with 50 foot-pounds, that's still only 2½-foot pounds of kinetic energy lost. I think that's a drop in the bucket under normal-hunting situations. You're going to shoot through a broadsided deer every time with either setup.

"Even on a broadsided, elk-sized animal, bowhunters should be able to shoot all the way through," he says. "The determining factor is arrow flight and broadhead configuration.

"To look at it another way, if you have an elk angling away, you hit him in the flank and the arrow goes up in front of the far shoulder," Adams says. "Let's say you get 30 inches in penetration with a 600-grain arrow. With a 400-grain arrow, if the elk is reasonably close, you're going to knock 5 percent off that 30 inches. That's not very much—only an inch and a half. I don't think an inch and a half on a quartering-away elk is enough to even worry about."

Adams says that in most situations, the difference between light and heavy arrows is grossly exaggerated.

"I like having medium to heavy arrows because the bow is qui-

AFC, makers of carbon arrow shafts since 1987, have introduced the AFC Carbon Camo shaft. This was the first attempt at camouflaging the otherwise solid black shafts.

eter,'' he says. ''That's because the arrow absorbs more energy, meaning less vibration coursing through the bow in the form of wasted energy. I get better arrow flight on average with a slower projectile that is medium to heavy in weight than I do with a lighter projectile that is medium to light in weight, all else being equal, with the same broadhead. There is less air friction on the blades of a broadhead flying 220 fps than there is on a broadhead flying 240 or 250 fps. Accuracy and a quieter bow are my two main reasons for shooting heavier shafts.

''There's one thing I want to say about energy,'' Adams continues. ''Lighter arrows peter out downrange more than heavy arrows. For example, the 400-grain arrow that is about 6 percent less effective one yard in front of the bow than the 600-grain arrow can be as much as 15 or 20 percent less effective at longer ranges, like 50 yards. You lose more kinetic energy downrange with a light projectile than you will with a heavier projectile, because it slows down faster. I've tested that in extreme cases with a 200-grain spread between arrow weights, and I've seen as much as a 20 percent difference at 50 yards. That's something else to consider.''

6

Selecting Effective Broadheads

Modern bowhunting tackle can quickly and efficiently kill big game. The key is selecting the best bow, the right arrow and the most effective broadhead. But how do you select the most effective broadhead for your setup and for the game you intend to hunt?

The broadhead you select must efficiently penetrate game and cut cleanly through organs and flesh. It must also maintain its structural integrity—not bend or break up—if it hits ribs or other bone. This broadhead also will determine, to some degree, arrow flight, arrow speed, kinetic energy and penetration potential. Of all the accessories available to bowhunters, few are more important. Only a broadhead can inflict the damage required to efficiently harvest big game. This, then, is one of the most important chapters in this book.

Fixed-Blade Or Replaceable-Blade Broadheads

Broadheads can be divided into two general categories: fixed blade or replaceable blade.

Blades on fixed-blade broadheads go all the way to the tip. These more traditional broadheads are also referred to as ''sharp-to-the-tip'' heads. They are known in the industry for their sturdy construction, and hunters generally believe that sharp-to-the-tip heads penetrate game better than replaceable-blade heads.

Myles Keller, who has taken 27 trophy whitetails with a bow, shoots sharp-to-the-tip broadheads. ''I have a tendency to shoot too far forward sometimes,'' he says. ''That's why I use a fixed-blade broadhead. It splits bones. It cuts on impact. And it produces very good penetration. I don't get tied up in the romanticism of sharpening my own broadheads. They have just been such good heads on bad hits that I go through with it because most times it's worth it.''

The hand sharpening required for sharp-to-the-tip broadheads is the major disadvantage. Bowhunters should sharpen their broadheads after every shot.

Replaceable-blade broadheads feature factory-sharpened replacement blades. After each shot, the bowhunter simply removes the old blades and slips replacement blades into the ferrule. Although hunters usually replace these blades after every shot, the blades can be resharpened, also.

A second advantage of using replaceable-blade heads is that vents are built into the blades. The vents reduce the blade's surface area, which also reduces the possibility of a replaceable-blade broadhead planing. Replaceable blades typically have less tendency to plane (veer off course). However, the tendency of both replaceable-blade heads and sharp-to-the-tip heads to plane can be controlled with the use of sufficient fletching and by properly tuning the bow.

Selecting The Proper Grain Weight

Broadheads are manufactured in various grain weights. Determining which weight is best for your hunting setup depends primarily upon your arrow shafts. For arrows weighing less than 500 grains, bowhunters should select a broadhead weighing 110 grains or less. This will result in the proper 7 to 10 percent-weight forward balance required for optimum arrow flight. For arrows weighing more than 500 grains, select a heavier broadhead, such as one weighing 125 or 140 grains.

To find your arrow's weight-forward balance point, attach a known grain-weight broadhead to the arrow shaft. Then find the point on the arrow at which the arrow balances. This point should be 7 to 10 percent of the arrow's length forward (toward the broadhead) from the middle of the arrow shaft. The balance point for a 30-inch arrow shaft, for example, should be from 2.8 to 3 inches forward from the middle of the arrow shaft.

When selecting the grain-weight broadhead, you should be sure that your bow and arrow will produce sufficient kinetic energy to drop the game you intend to hunt. A general rule-of-thumb calls for a minimum of 40 foot-pounds of kinetic energy for deer-sized animals and 50 foot-pounds for big game larger than deer. To determine your ar-

Despite all of the advancements in bow and arrow design, it is the broadhead that ultimately inflicts the fatal blow. Proper broadhead selection impacts arrow penetration, speed and trajectory.

row's kinetic energy, use the formula listed in Chapter 3.

Arrow velocity and total arrow weight can usually be determined at your local pro shop. The shop's staff should also be able to show you how to increase the kinetic energy of your setup, if needed.

Broadheads And Arrow Flight

As mentioned earlier, the general belief is that broadheads with vented blades fly consistently truer on average than non-vented broadheads. To better control broadhead flight under less-than-perfect conditions, bowhunters should try using 5-inch helical fletch. This is especially true of bowhunters shooting some of the larger sharp-to-the-tip heads.

Whichever broadhead design you select, practice shooting it before you go hunting. Broadheads don't always group the same as field points. Group size may be similar, but point of impact may be substantially different. Shoot your broadheads and adjust your sights accordingly.

How Many Blades Are Best?

Broadheads carry anywhere from two to six blades. Generally, the fewer the blades, the greater the penetration—all else being equal. All else being equal, a 3-blade broadhead should penetrate deeper than a 4-blade head. However, a disadvantage would be the possibility of a reduced blood trail.

"What I don't like about two-blade broadheads is the definite difference in the amount of blood on the ground," says Chuck Adams. "A two-blade broadhead cuts a slit instead of a hole. I'm convinced that the slit seals up more easily and affects blood loss. That can be very important in the deep woods where tracking can be a problem."

Chuck uses two-blade heads when he needs a deep penetrating broadhead for thick-skinned or large big game with well-protected vitals. "When I bowhunted in Africa," Chuck said. "I took two-blade broadheads to shoot larger animals and to test penetration depth. For example, a sable antelope is not a big animal—it probably weighs 500 pounds. But a sable's hide averages three-quarters of an inch thick over the vital zone. Because of that, I wanted two-blade broadheads for deeper penetration. And I definitely got that. I shot clean through everything I hit with a two-blade broadhead. The arrow came out the other side and went into the dirt every time."

A Broadhead's Affect On Penetration

According to Adams and Mullaney, the top two factors affecting

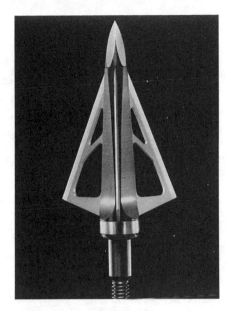

Replaceable-blade broadheads like this Thunderhead 100 are factory sharpened. An advantage of vented, replaceable-blade broadheads is that they are less likely to plane in flight.

arrow penetration potential are the broadhead and the hunting arrow's kinetic energy.

Adams has conducted considerable research to determine how the design of a broadhead influences penetration potential. His tests were conducted on dead animals and on green cow hides.

''The results are very consistent from one test to another,'' he explains. ''The least sure-fire test method is shooting through animals, because you have ribs and you can't shoot your broadhead through the same place twice. But I have found that any broadhead with a cutting nose, such as the old Bear Razorhead, the new Razorhead stainless steel, the Zwickey Black Diamond, the Hoyt Top Cut or Bow Bullet, the Bohning Blazer or the Satellite Titan, penetrates deeper.'' Adams has found that those cutting-nose broadheads give him 25 percent more penetration depth than a pyramid point or a nose-cone-type broadhead, all else being equal.

The bigger the nose cone, or the area in front of the blades, the lower the penetration potential, Adams says. His experiments show that a bowhunter can lose up to 45 percent of overall penetration depth depending upon how much surface area is in front of the blades.

A chisel point or pyramid point, he found, did much better at penetrating. However, these chisel or pyramid points did not come close to the penetration achieved by a true cutting-nose broadhead. ''A cutting-nose broadhead, in my experiments, recorded 25 percent

Broadhead design directly affects penetration, according to Chuck Adams. He has found that sharp-to-the-tip broadheads (left) penetrate better than nose-cone (center) or pyramid-point (right) broadheads.

more penetration than a chisel-nose broadhead,'' he says. ''It varies with nose-cone broadheads, but we're talking probably 35 percent less penetration with a nose-cone broadhead than with a cutting-nose broadhead.''

Adams supports these findings with this example: ''David File, a long-time employee of Easton Aluminum, and I went on a pig hunt in northern California. Dave shot a big boar and we tested penetration with shots behind that boar's shoulder with three nose-cone broadheads, two chisel-point broadheads and two cutting-nose broadheads. The cutting-nose broadheads were the Bear Razorhead No. 1 and the Zwickey Black Diamond No. 2. One of the nose-cone broadheads that had a large nose was actually bouncing off the pig at about 25 yards. Now, remember that pigs have a nylon-type callous shield over the ribs that is very tough to penetrate. You wouldn't bounce an arrow off a deer. But one was bouncing off that pig. The average nose-cone broadhead was penetrating about 6 inches into the pig. The chisel-nose broadheads were going in a bit deeper, about 8 to 10 inches.

''By comparison, the cutting-nose broadheads would penetrate completely through the pig, which was about 15 inches from side to side. About half the time, the Zwickey broadhead (the four-blade Eskimo) was not only penetrating out the other side, the arrow was actually exiting the pig and burying in the dirt on the other side. The Bear Razorhead was almost doing that. I have never figured out why it didn't penetrate quite as well. I think it may be the little ridges on the front of the ferrule where they attach the blade. There is some friction associated with those. That is the only thing I can figure out. The differences were dramatic. And David File, who was a nose-cone-type broadhead guy at the time, immediately switched to a cutting-nose broadhead.''

All these broadheads tested were of the same grain weight, Adams says, and the bow was properly tuned.

''I do want to say that any aerodynamically sound broadhead—a broadhead that flies well, and is well constructed and is sharp—will bag deer-sized animals and smaller. I think the differences in penetration with nose-cone or pyramid-point or cutting-nose broadheads come more into play with larger animals like elk or moose or maybe big black bear. I don't think anybody should worry about shooting a Muzzy or a Thunderhead if he is hunting deer-sized animals and smaller. With larger animals, I begin worrying about the difference. On the other hand, if you lose 25 percent of your penetrating ability in the broadhead design, it's the difference between a 60- and an 80-

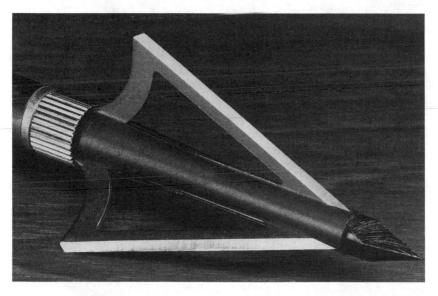

This Bohning Zapper weighs 125 grains, which is the most popular broadhead weight. Choose a weight that moves the arrow's balance point 7 to 10 percent forward from the shaft's exact middle.

pound draw weight bow. That's something to think about.''

Mullaney, however, doesn't completely agree with Adams' findings. In a ''Technical Topics'' column in a bowhunting publication, Mullaney examined the issue of broadhead penetration potential. He tested 18 different broadheads, including sharp-to-the-tip broadheads and cone or pyramid-tip broadheads. For these tests, Mullaney used a bow shooting machine to shoot the broadheads under controlled conditions into ethafoam targets.

''This material [ethafoam] is sufficiently uniform so that in nine shots with the same arrow and broadhead combination, the depth of penetration achieved will not vary more than $5/16$ inch for all nine shots, with average penetration in the neighborhood of 12 inches,'' he wrote. '' ... It is, without question, an excellent target medium to compare the penetration capabilities of different types of broadheads.

''After a thorough analysis of the results of the test,'' Mullaney explained, ''I was forced to the conclusion that, as a type, blade-to-the-tip broadheads do not demonstrate greater penetration capability than broadheads with replaceable blades. There is greater difference in penetration capability due to the basic design of the broadhead than there is as a result of whether or not the blades extend all the way to the tip.''

Keeping Broadheads Razor Sharp

No matter which style and grain-weight broadhead is selected, the blades must be kept razor sharp. A dull broadhead, no matter what its penetration potential, will not penetrate nearly as well as it should.

Fixed blades and replaceable blades may need to be touched up occasionally. A honing stone is the most common way to touch up a broadhead. However, pocket-sized cross sticks can also keep a razor's edge on your blades. Most stones and small cross sticks are small enough to slip into the corner of a day pack, or carry in your tackle box of bowhunting supplies. Remember that simply taking a broadhead-tipped arrow out of a quiver and putting it back in is enough to dull the blades.

Razor-sharp broadheads are sharp enough to shave the hair off your arm. That test could be hazardous, so another way is to lightly draw the broadhead over a rubber band. A razor-sharp head should slice through the rubber band with little pressure applied.

Protecting Razor-Sharp Broadheads

A game animal's hide is not the only skin a razor-sharp broad-

The blades on a broadhead should be touched up after each use. A honing stone or these cross sticks can be used on both fixed-blade and replaceable-blade broadheads to keep blades razor sharp.

head will cut with ease. Treat broadheads with respect. Use the broadhead wrench supplied by the broadhead manufacturer to put them on and take them off your arrows; never try to unscrew a broadhead with your hand.

When you're hunting, keep all broadhead-tipped arrows in a bow or hip quiver where the broadheads are enclosed in a sturdy, solid hood. Many state-sponsored bowhunter education instructors encourage bowhunters to keep their arrows in such a quiver even when still-hunting.

If you must fly to your hunting destination, or drive a long distance, it may not be possible to have your broadheads attached to arrows. Small, sturdy plastic tackle boxes are specially designed to keep the broadheads organized and protected for extended travel. You can use these tackle boxes to store extra broadheads in hunting camp or at home.

7

Outfitting Your Bow

A ccessories can help bowhunters shoot more accurately, consistently and comfortably. Sights give archers aiming points at pre-set distances. Quivers hold arrows safely and within easy reach. Arrow rests provide consistent platforms from which to launch arrows. The list of potential accessories goes on, including peep sights, stabilizers, release aids, overdraws and more. Whatever a bowhunter desires, chances are that there is an accessory to meet that need.

All bowhunting accessories, however, must be purchased prudently because most accessories can be a help or a hindrance. Even though designed to improve accuracy or ability, each can be a potential source of game-spooking noise. And each accessory means one more piece of equipment to be carried into the field. Bowhunting, a sport of implied simplicity that brings forth images of Robin Hood or an American Indian drawing back a slick bow devoid of complicated attachments, can suddenly become a gadget-riddled sport. Of course, that can be half the fun ... sometimes.

Most bowhunters experiment with components to accessorize their setups. The secret is to keep this question in mind when outfitting your hunting bow: Will this product improve my ability to draw, aim and/or release an accurate shot at game? The answer will not always be *yes*. It is extremely important to remember this question or you may end up a slave to your accessories rather than the master of your bow. Chuck Adams says, ''I firmly believe that the simplest

Sight pins in a hunter's sight are used as solid aiming points for several predetermined distances. For example, if you estimate the animal is 20 yards away, then you would use the sight pin that had been zeroed in at that distance as your aiming point.

setup that works is the best.'' Here, then, are the most practical bow-hunting accessories.

Sights For Improved Accuracy

Sights give a bowhunter solid aiming points from several distances. Bow-mounted sights typically feature as many as five aiming points which can be adjusted to correspond with set distances. Determine the distance to the target, then select the nearest corresponding aiming pin. Some bowhunters are successful instinctive shooters. But most bowhunters use sights. Sights improve accuracy by providing a reliable aiming point with little or no guesswork. In those high-pressure situations when big game is within bow range, you don't need the extra burden of determining whether you should aim high, low or somewhere in-between. When a big-game animal is 20 yards away, you should be able to put your 20-yard pin on the animal's vitals and release. Simple enough. To shoot without sights would be like trying to shoot a rifle without a scope or without open sights. Shooting a broadhead-tipped arrow at a game animal requires a sighting system for pinpoint accuracy for most bowhunters.

Pin or Crosshair Sights. There are two basic sighting systems: pin and crosshair. The pin sight is the most popular and features up to five pins which can be independently adjusted for windage and elevation. Place the "head" or ball of the pin on the target and release.

A crosshair sight uses several horizontal and one vertical line to form crosshair aiming points. Windage on all five settings can be adjusted by moving the vertical axis.

Both sighting systems work. Both are effective. Which one you shoot is a matter of personal preference. Whichever type of sight you choose, however, can be a notorious source of bow noise. Be sure to tighten all pins or crosshairs. A sight that dovetails into the bow will fit more securely.

Peep Sight. Although a peep sight is not required, it can complete your sighting system by firming up your anchor point. A peep becomes the rear sight of your aiming system. It's like aiming a rifle with front and rear sights, as opposed to aiming a shotgun with just a front bead. Many hunters, including the author, have used a peep sight for years and would not plan to hunt again without one. A peep helps the shooter draw into a quick, solid anchor and lock onto the target quickly once he is properly anchored.

Two basic considerations regarding peep sights are aperture and string rotation. Many peep sights have a small-diameter opening. Even though this can be beneficial with most targets, it can be a prob-

Most bownhunters find that their accuracy improves when they use a peep sight. If you use one, make sure it's large enough to transmit enough light in low-light conditions.

lem when you're shooting in low light conditions or at dark-colored animals.

Chuck Adams says he has been shooting a peep sight on targets and game for more than 10 years. ''I've tried it both ways, and a peep sight definitely improves accuracy,'' he says. ''If you shoot a peep sight, however, you need an aperture large enough to get good light transmission to the eye. In my mind that means an aperture of at least ⅛ inch in diameter. I prefer ³⁄₁₆-inch aperture.''

The other consideration with a peep sight is string rotation, especially with finger shooters who may rotate the string slightly when drawing. That string rotation places the peep out of alignment, making it difficult or impossible to see through. One option for accommodating string rotation is to offset your peep with the bow drawn down. Then, when you draw back and rotate the string, the peep will align straight with your eye. First, determine how much you rotate the string. If you consistently rotate the string to the right 90 degrees, for example, offset the peep 90 degrees to the left while the bow is drawn down. Of course, this requires drawing the string with the same rotation every time, even while hunting in extremely cold or hot weather.

The second option for correcting string rotation is to install an umbilical cord running from the peep sight to the cable assembly in order to keep the peep facing forward. "For the average person, I think an umbilical-type peep of some kind is best," says Adams. "You can get kits that work with any peep style that allows you to attach surgical tubing to the peep area and to the cable that rises."

Umbilical-type positioners that attach to the inside of the top bow limb are available. However, this extra tubing can be a source of more bow noise, and the tubing can wear at stress points and require maintenance. One that attaches to the cable will do the same job with less noise and maintenance. Just be sure to attach it to the cable that goes up when you draw.

Arrow Quivers

Bow-mounted quivers are no-nonsense products. Quivers hold arrows securely within easy reach and protect broadheads. Bow-mounted quivers are attached to the bow with screw-in bolts or a snap-on bracket. Broadheads are protected in sturdy, foam-filled hoods. Quivers typically grip arrows with rubber in front of the fletch.

Bow-mounted quivers can hold up to eight arrows (with broadheads attached) safely and within easy reach by the bow-hunter. The quiver should have a hard-shelled broadhead hood.

Fasten your quiver securely to reduce game-spooking noise. Also, be sure to practice and tune your bow with your quiver and arrows attached. A quiver with a handful of arrows will add weight to your bow. Plus, a full quiver can influence point of impact. This is because the attached arrows, weighing 500 to 600 grains each, can change the feel of your bow.

Or if you want to eliminate this problem altogether, choose a hip quiver. Like bow quivers, hip quivers have a protective head and gripping rubber snaps. The advantage for the shooter is the arrows do not add weight to the bow.

Finger Tabs And Release Aids

Finger tabs, shooting gloves or mechanical release aids can help you release cleanly and consistently. Finger tabs and shooting gloves are typically leather. Both are simple and straightforward. (Always carry an extra finger tab or shooting glove with you just in case yours rips or is misplaced.) They are inexpensive and lightweight.

There are three release-aid designs: rope, caliper and ball bearing. I have been shooting with a release aid for several years and doubt whether I would shoot fingers again—at least for hunting. A rope release significantly improved my accuracy, especially when shooting with a 65 percent let-off bow.

A mechanical release lets go of the bowstring consistently regardless of the conditions in the field. During a late-October whitetailed deer bowhunt, the ambient temperature was close to 10 degrees below zero; the windchill was 40 degrees below zero. Although I was wearing wool gloves and Gore-Tex mittens, my fingers still were extremely cold. I doubt whether I could have released a bowstring, using a finger tab or shooting glove. However, the mechanical release aid functioned perfectly. It released the string perfectly when an 8-point whitetail came within 20 yards of my tree stand. A friend hunting another valley that same day shot at a doe 25 yards away; but he didn't connect. He is a finger shooter and had to shed his protective mitten as the deer approached. He said his fingers nearly froze before the deer gave him the opportunity for a shot. Release aids do not get numb or stiff in the cold. Nor do they get sweaty and slippery under hot, humid conditions.

Rope-design release aids are built around a thin, flexible rope that attaches from the outside inward, exiting the front of the release side by side.

A caliper release features pincers or "alligator jaws" which grip the bowstring, minimizing bowstring torque; ball-bearing release

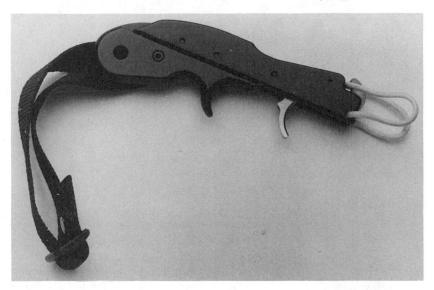

This Browning Rope Trigger is one example of the three basic mechanical release aids. The other two are the caliper and the ball bearing release. Your choice is largely a matter of personal preference.

aids utilize two ball bearings for a smooth bowstring release.

Although a release can improve accuracy, it has two disadvantages. First, a release makes you dependent on one more accessory. If something happened to your release in the field, it would be difficult to switch to finger shooting without losing accuracy. Always carry two releases with you when hunting. If one malfunctions or is left behind, you can continue hunting the way you are accustomed. Second, mechanical release aids are noisier than fingers. This added bow noise increases the chances of an animal "jumping the string."

When selecting a release, look for one with an adjustable trigger and a head that prevents the release from putting torque on the string. Also, choose one that is comfortable to shoot. If your release has a wrist strap, make sure that the material does not dig into your skin. If it does, it certainly will be uncomfortable to use during extended practice sessions.

Arrow Rests

There are various arrow rests on the market. Most provide a consistent platform for launching arrows.

"There are a lot of arrow rests out there," says Terry Ragsdale, three-time World Archery Champion and four-time National Field

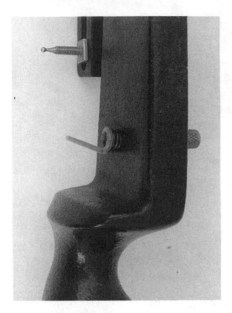

Shoot-around rests are simple, effective and inexpensive. They also are the preferred rest of a number of well-known bowhunters. This Springie rest has a Teflon sleeve for quieter operation.

Archery Association Champion. "Go to any shoot or tournament and you will see many different arrow rests and they all seem to work fine. Which arrow rest is best is really a matter of whatever tickles an archer's fancy—whatever he likes to shoot the best."

Although many micro-adjustable, shoot-through arrow rests are available, most top shooters agree with Chuck Adams' reasoning that " ... the simplest setup that works is the best."

Ragsdale, for instance, shoots a simple Springie rest. "I just put a teflon sleeve on it to prevent any noise," he says.

Bob Fratzke, who has taken over 20 trophy-class whitetails, shoots the J-2 arrow rest from Jennings. "I can shoot the best rest the manufacturers make," says Fratzke, "but the one I'm shooting is the J-2. You don't even have to use a button with it. I even shoot them in tournaments." Fratzke invented Winona Camo Systems and is a member of the Bear Archery Pro Staff.

Another fairly inexpensive rest is the Centerest Flipper Arrowrest from New Archery Products. The Centerest features a built-in cushion plunger action and can be quickly replaced in the field. The rest has ample centershot adjustment, making it adaptable for both standard and offset risers. Replacement rests are available and installation takes about two minutes. The Centerest comes complete with extra sleeves and felt pads for quieting your rest.

Arrow rests go up from there in price, adjustability and complexity. I shoot a more complex rest with cushion plunger. Why? Because one day a salesman at a local archery pro shop told me it was one of the best rests on the market. I had to find out, so I bought one, shot it and liked it. Since then, I have used that rest on hunts for deer, elk and pronghorn and have been pleased with its performance. Arrow rest selection is largely a matter of personal preference.

Arm Guard

The arm guard protects the inside forearm of your bow hand from being slapped by the bowstring as it travels forward. Experienced bowhunters usually have learned to hold their bow in such a way so that there won't be contact between bowstring and forearm. However, an arm guard is inexpensive insurance, plus it can keep a shirt- or coat-sleeve from getting in the way of the string as it travels forward. If the bowstring makes contact with clothes as it travels forward, the contact will adversely affect arrow flight.

Bow Sling

Bow slings are simple, inexpensive and effective. A bow sling allows you to open up your bow hand when shooting so you don't put torque or twist on the bow. The bow sling prevents the bow from slip-

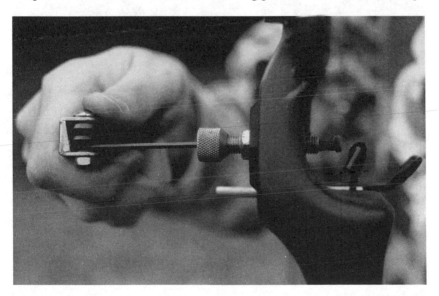

Shoot-through rests sport more high-tech adjustments than the shoot-around rests, and they're more expensive. Moleskin has been added to this Huntmaster 2000 rest to silence the draw and release.

If you don't use an arm guard, an occasion probably will arise when you wish you had used one. It also helps to keep loose sleeves out of the way when you're releasing an arrow.

ping from your grasp after you have released the bowstring.

String Silencers

String silencers quiet your bow and reduce game-spooking bow noise. Both rubber cat whiskers and yarn-like puff balls are inexpensive yet effective. They should be attached to the bowstring at least 6 inches from each axle. Research by Saunders Archery Company, a silencer manufacturer, showed an average bowstring without silencers vibrated 47 times after each shot (One vibration equaled a movement of at least ¼ inch.) A bowstring with the least effective string silencers vibrated 12 times; the most effective string silencers reduced bowstring vibrations from 47 to three.

Stabilizer

Bow stabilizers can quiet your hunting bow and reduce game-spooking noise. When a bowstring is released, not all of the bow's energy is transferred to the arrow. Remaining energy courses through the setup and produces game-spooking noise. A bow stabilizer acts like a shock absorber, absorbing the vibration and energy.

Most serious target archers use stabilizers to help balance the bow, says Ragsdale. "Stabilizers may not necessarily increase the accuracy of a bow, but they do help to balance and make a bow stand up the way you want it to when you release the arrow," he says. "On hunting bows, I do not notice any difference in terms of accuracy whether I shoot with a stabilizer or without."

Overdraws

Overdraws are popular replacements for rests. A bowhunter can use a shorter arrow with an overdraw. The overdraw moves the arrow rest back toward the shooter and away from its normal position on the bow handle. A shorter arrow shaft weighs less and flies faster with a flatter trajectory. That is the advantage of an overdraw.

Depending upon the overdraw model, total arrow length can be shortened by up to 5 inches. Also, most overdraws accept a variety of arrow rests. They also have a protective shelf or guard that shields the bow hand from the broadhead.

Rangefinding Devices

Bowhunters spend hours sighting in and tuning their bows. They

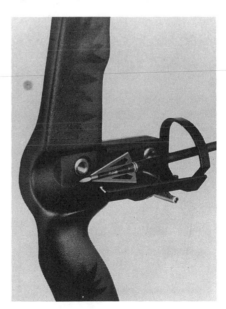

With an overdraw like this Stealth Overdraw from Bear Archery, a bowhunter can shoot shorter, lighter arrows for more speed and a flatter trajectory, compensating for range-estimation errors.

set their sights at various distances, and make sure their arrows hit the target. During the hunting season, bowhunters take these accurate set-ups into the woods. Of course, distances in the field are not marked. Thankfully, most bowhunters can accurately pace off the distance to a scrape, game trail or wallow.

However, shooting opportunities can sometimes unfold quickly, and there is no time to pace off the distance. Also, pacing off shooting lanes from your tree stand or ground blind may be accurate, but it can also disperse your scent—that's something successful bowhunters avoid. These situations call for a rangefinding device that can measure the distance to an object accurately and quickly. Most rangefinders are lightweight and easy to use.

8

Tuning Your Hunting Rig

Although I hate to admit it, this is true: After three years and two bows, I finally learned how to properly tune my hunting rig. It was simple. And once I learned, I laughed. I could have saved myself a lot of trouble and a good dose of frustration, even a smidgen of anger, if I knew then what I know now about bow tuning.

When I first started bowhunting, here's what happened: The salesperson installed the nock on my bowstring. Then he installed my arrow rest and sight. He eye-balled the rest and nock alignment, made a few adjustments, and handed me the finished product.

I took the bow home, confident that it was now ready to be sighted in. So with a handful of properly sized arrows and my new bow I went down to the bow range. Of course, if the arrow hit too low, I lowered my sight pin. If the arrow hit right, I moved my sight to the right. It was a fairly simple process, I thought. But sometimes it was frustrating. Sometimes, I would do everything right and I would still get mediocre groupings, especially compared to the other shooters.

With that same bow, I shot a relatively small-bodied game animal, broadside from 25 yards. The arrow penetrated one lung but did not go through the animal as I had expected it would. And, unfortunately, a second shot was required about five minutes later. We were hunting open farm country and could see the buck, making it an easy stalk.

Later, I tried to figure out why my arrow hadn't gone completely through the small-bodied animal—especially at 25 yards. At the time, I was shooting a 65-pound draw-weight bow, 31-inch 2219 XX75s and 125-grain broadheads. Surely that setup should produce sufficient kinetic energy for a pass-through shot. But it didn't. And I still couldn't figure out why.

Then, one day a fellow bowhunter said he had just paper-tested his bow and significantly improved his grouping.

"Paper tested?" I asked.

And so he explained.

The following Saturday I went back to the archery shop where I had purchased that second bow. "I want to paper-test my bow," I said, as I entered the store.

The pro shop staffer nodded and led me down a stairway into the basement. At one end of what looked like a long closet about 4 feet wide and 20 feet long was a target. Between the target and me was a taut sheet of paper held in place by a metal picture frame.

I set up my equipment and shot through the paper. After two shots, it was obvious that my bow needed to be tuned. "You want a very clean hole," the staffperson said. My arrows were leaving a 2-inch tear in the paper.

After 10 minutes and some basic adjustments, my arrows were flying perfectly through the paper. We tested and adjusted my setup until it shot consistently through paper from distances of 5, 10 and 15 feet away.

Why didn't my arrow go completely through that small-bodied game animal? My sights were on the target. And my setup should have been producing sufficient kinetic energy. The only reasonable explanation is that I was losing penetration potential because of sloppy arrow flight. Instead of the broadhead-tipped arrow passing clean through, it may have been pushed at an angle through that animal. Sloppy arrow flight probably was literally squandering valuable kinetic energy.

Of course, an arrow shot from a properly tuned bow makes better use of its kinetic energy (penetration potential). The reason is that an arrow shot from a properly tuned bow will fly straight; an arrow shot from a bow which is not tuned properly will fishtail, porpoise or wag. When a sloppy-flying arrow hits the target, a portion of its kinetic energy is wasted laterally. An arrow shot from a properly tuned bow should penetrate like a nail being driven straight into wood; an arrow shot from an improperly tuned bow penetrates like a nail being driven sideways into wood.

The process for properly tuning your hunting bow is fairly

Here's the kind of situation you'll encounter when you go to your local archery pro shop to paper test your bow. The paper should be a minimum of five yards in front of the bow. Also remember to have a target butt behind the paper.

Interpreting Paper Tears–1

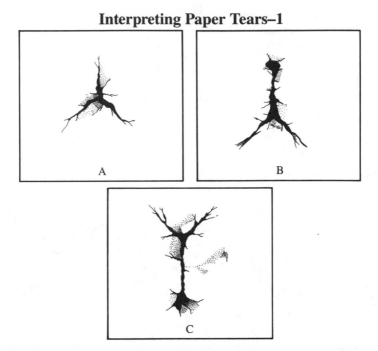

A paper test of a properly tuned bow should produce an apparent bullet hole with three fletch marks (A). Vertical tears indicate the bowstring nock is either too low (B) or too high (C). Move the nock ¹⁄₁₆ inch either up or down and shoot again.

straightforward. It does not take an immense amount of time, but it does require some basic information and some practical solutions. Now, onto the basics. (It's assumed you are shooting properly spined arrow shafts from a bow with correct draw length and desired draw weight.)

Outfit Your Bow As If To Hunt

Before tuning your hunting rig, outfit your bow just as you would for hunting. Attach the bow quiver with as many arrows as you would normally carry into the field. Attach the sight, string silencers and arrow rest and anything else you have on the bow when hunting.

Bow-mounted accessories can change the weight of a bow, and the added weight change can affect the point of arrow impact. If your bow is tuned without the quiver attached, you should hunt with it that way in the field. A quiver, complete with eight, 500-grain arrows, will add weight to one side of your bow, which could affect shot placement. Strap on everything that you want on your bow.

Also, be certain that your bowstring nock is properly aligned. Don't just eye-ball it and figure that's close enough. The bottom of the nock should be ⅜ inch above the line from the arrow rest to the bowstring.

Paper Test Your Hunting Arrow Shaft

The best place to paper-test your setup is at a local archery pro shop. Visit the shop before the start of hunting season. Everybody likes to shop right before the season begins, and archery pro shop experts are usually willing to help. However, during busy times they are often required to be on the floor assisting customers who want to buy equipment, rather than assisting shooters who want to tune their hunting setup. So, get started early, and contact local shops to see if they can help you paper-test your setup.

Paper testing is a simple process. Basically, you shoot an arrow

Interpreting Paper Tears–2

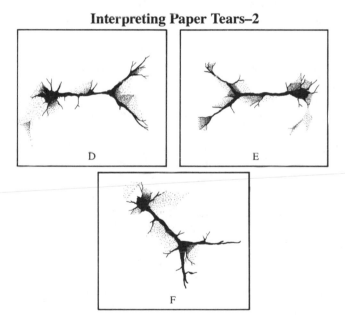

Horizontal tears indicate either rest alignment problems or an improperly spined shaft. Right-handed shooters should move the arrow rest in toward the bow handle to correct a tear to the right (D) and move the rest out to correct a tear to the left (E). A diagonal tear (F) indicates combined problems; solve the vertical problem and then correct the horizontal problem.

through a taut, upright sheet of paper that is at least 5 feet away. Be sure that there is a solid target behind the paper to stop your arrow. When the arrow passes through the taut paper, it leaves a telltale clue as to its flight. For instance, if it is flying nose down and tail up, the arrow will leave a solid hole with a tear that goes up from the hole. The goal is to get a bullet-shaped hole with three fletch marks fanning out from it. That means the arrow and the fletch went straight through the same hole.

When paper-testing your hunting rig, make only one adjustment at a time. After it's made, shoot again so you can see and judge the effect of that change. Nock point changes, for example, should be made in ⅟16-inch increments.

Correcting Vertical Tears. A vertical tear, whether running up or down from the arrow's entry hole, can be corrected by adjusting the nocking point.

If the fletch cuts through the paper below the arrow shaft hole, the nocking point is too low. Raise it by ⅟16 inch, and shoot again. Continue to raise the nock in ⅟16-inch increments and continue to test shoot after each adjustment until the shaft leaves the desired, clean bullet hole with three fletch marks.

If the fletch cuts through the paper above the arrow point, however, the nocking point is too high. Lower it ⅟16 inch and shoot again. Continue to adjust and shoot until the arrow shaft leaves the desired hole in the paper.

Nocks on the bowstring can be moved in one of two ways. The most common way is loosening the nock with a special pliers and trying to move it the correct distance up or down. It can be difficult, however, to see if the nocking point has moved ⅟16 inch. Sometimes, if the nocking is too loose, it will slide a full half inch or more up or down the string. When this happens, you must start over.

The second way to adjust bowstring nock location is a simple and effective method. If the bowstring nock is first placed in approximately the correct location, it can be adjusted into the correct location by tightening one limb bolt a quarter turn at a time and loosening the other limb bolt an equal amount. For raising the nock, for instance, tighten the upper limb bolt one-quarter turn and loosen the lower limb bolt one-quarter turn. This method may require some trial-and-error experimentation to master because the size of eccentrics and axle-to-axle length varies from bow to bow. However, it can be an easy way to adjust nock location without loosening your bowstring nock and possibly damaging your bowstring. Both methods work. Find out which works best for you and stick with it.

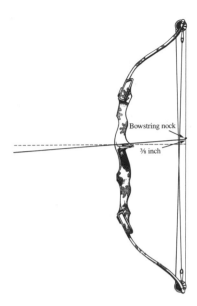

As a starting point, the nock point should be set ⅜ inch above the horizontal line through the rest (broken line). The arrow then will be at a slightly downward angle (solid line). Then, make your adjustments.

Correcting Horizontal Tears. A horizontal tear, whether left or right of the hole, made by the arrow's point can be corrected by horizontally adjusting the arrow rest's position. Tears can also be caused by an arrow shaft not properly spined for your setup.

If the fletch tears to the right of the arrow-point hole, right-hand shooters should move the arrow rest in toward the bow handle less than 1/16 of an inch. Then shoot again. If there is only slight improvement, move the arrow rest in toward the bow handle again. Then shoot. If moving the arrow rest in doesn't correct the problem, your shaft may be too stiff for your setup.

To weaken a shaft which is too stiff, one of three things can be done: increase draw weight, increase field-point weight or buy weaker-spined arrow shafts. Of course, the first two are the least expensive and easiest. Sometimes, a few pounds in peak draw weight solves the problem. Other times, shooting heavier field points or broadheads works. And, sometimes combining these first two options weakens the shaft sufficiently. When you first start increasing draw weight, increase slowly—a pound or two at a time.

As mentioned before, make only one adjustment at a time. Don't change draw weight and switch to heavier field points without paper testing what impact the increase in draw weight had on the arrow flight. The third option is to shoot heavier shafts. This should be a last resort. Buying new arrows can be expensive. But sometimes that's the only solution. Consult an arrow shaft selection chart at the pro shop to determine which shaft you should shoot. If you do purchase new shafts, bring your bow's draw weight down to the level that is most comfortable for you.

A horizontal tear from the fletch to the left of the arrow-point hole can be corrected by moving the arrow rest out away from the bow handle. As stated above, move the arrow shaft slightly, then paper-test the bow each time. If it does not pass the paper test, you may be shooting shafts that are too weak for your setup.

To stiffen a weak shaft, decrease the peak draw weight, decrease field-point weight or purchase stiffer arrow shafts. Decreasing peak draw weight or decreasing field-point weight is the easiest and least expensive. And again, make only one correction at a time. Purchasing new arrow shafts can be expensive, but it can also be the only solution. Consult a shaft selection chart for a stiffer hunting arrow shaft.

Correcting Diagonal Tears. Sometimes paper-testing will reveal that more than one factor is out of whack. If this happens, simply use—one at a time—the steps listed in this chapter. First correct the vertical problem by adjusting your nocking point, then correct the horizontal problem by moving the rest.

The hard work is done. To fine-tune your hunting rig, step back another 10 feet and start again to paper-test your setup. Adjustments, where required, should be minimal at this stage.

9

Traditional Bowhunting

Despite a compound bow's inherent advantages—faster arrow speed, more kinetic energy and lower holding weight—an estimated 12 percent of bowhunters prefer traditional bowhunting equipment. Traditionalists typically prefer recurves or longbows, shoot instinctively rather than with sights, and shoot fingers rather than mechanical release aids; they do not take advantage of the technological advances and improvements in bows and bowhunting accessories. One great thing about bowhunting is that the sport is large enough to accommodate everyone—from the most high-tech shooters to traditionalists who want archery to be a simple sport. This chapter examines the philosophy behind traditional archery, as well as equipment and performance.

Earl Hoyt built his first bow back in the late 1920s by following the instructions described in his Boy Scout handbook. He used hickory wood on his first bow, and he was hooked for life. Today, Earl Hoyt is one of bowhunting's last great patriarchs. During the past 70-odd years Hoyt has known most of the bowhunting greats, including Fred Bear and Howard Hill. And he witnessed the changes in bow construction and materials. Today, of course, bows are manufactured using more than just hickory wood, and the techniques used to make today's bows are more complicated and sophisticated than the instructions in any Boy Scout manual. But despite these changes and advancements in technology and materials, Hoyt still enjoys shooting and talking about traditional bowhunting equipment.

Traditional bowhunters, Hoyt explains, enjoy the nostalgia and mystique surrounding a bowhunt with traditional archery equipment. There is a sense of going back to the simple ingredients of a bow and arrow, hunter and game.

"We started building traditional bows in the 1930s out of Osage orange and yew wood," Hoyt recalls. Some archers and bowhunters placed rawhide on the backs of bows to increase their durability. When fiberglass was invented in the 1950s manufacturers, including Hoyt, started to laminate fiberglass to wood to produce smoother, faster and more durable limbs.

"Such limbs were far superior in performance and consistency," says Hoyt. "We were building traditional equipment with modern materials, but we were still constructing what are known as traditional bows. There were some companies out there that continued to manufacture wood bows, but not many. And unless you are really a purist, you shoot laminate bows. There is a great difference between the performance of a wood bow and a bow with laminated limbs." Hoyt, a competitive archer and bowhunter, has taken 15 deer with traditional archery equipment.

Owen Jeffrey, who once worked for Hoyt but now owns Jeffrey Archery in South Carolina, outlines the construction techniques used with most traditional bows. Jeffrey says traditional take-down recurves sport laminated wood handles and limbs with a wood core and fiberglass on the front and on the back of the bow. Bowstring material is the same as what is used on modern compound bows, either Dacron or Fast-Flight.

Jeffrey manufactures traditional bows for several major bow companies. He also makes custom bows, as well as replicas. Like Hoyt, Jeffrey is an avid traditional bowhunter. He has been bowhunting since 1950, and he reports that he has harvested more than 70 deer and more than 40 wild hogs with one particular traditional bow. "It's a 40-inch long Jeffrey bow with a 50-pound draw weight," says Jeffrey. "Most people strive for a high peak draw weight. But placing the arrow correctly is more important than how much weight you draw back. And how cleanly an arrow leaves the bow is even more important." An arrow can expend much of its kinetic energy attempting to push through the animal if it is not flying true.

Jeffrey tunes his bows by watching his arrows fly when they leave his bow. Of course, this is a skill he developed over the years. Most bowhunters will need to paper-test their traditional bow from a variety of distances to properly tune the bow. To the bowhunter shoot-

Despite the seeming advantages of the compound bow, an estimated 12 percent of the nation's bowhunters opt for shooting so-called traditional equipment—either a long bow or a recurve.

ing compound equipment and a sophisticated arrow rest, it might seem difficult to properly tune a traditional bow. But Jeffrey, who shoots with a finger-type arrow rest, says that brace height, nocking point and bow hand grip can be adjusted in order to properly tune a traditional bow.

"By and large," Jeffrey says, "traditional bowhunters are a little more sophisticated in their pursuit of the game animal. They try to emulate the ways of the early bowhunters. The traditional bowhunter accepts the fact that he has a limited effective range and that he must draw back a relatively long bow. However, there is also an ego involved. And some traditional archers ... look down at people who use new or improved equipment." The appeal in traditional bowhunting is a combination of these factors, according to Jeffrey.

Hoyt describes bowhunters who favor traditional archery equipment this way: "With traditional bowhunters there is a sense of nostalgia and mystique. There is also a sense of returning to and hunting with a more primitive weapon. And while the concept of a bow and arrow is simple, the equipment they are using is effective." Hoyt's company, Sky Archery, manufactures a traditional bow that achieves an arrow speed of 204 feet per second at Archery Manufacturers Organization (AMO) standards (60-pound draw weight, 30-inch draw and 540-grain arrow).

An arrow speed of 204 fps is fast enough to compete with many compound bows on the market today. Many high-tech compounds, for example, at AMO standards, achieve an arrow speed of 210 through 240 fps.

Despite the advantages of traditional laminate-limb bows—or compound bows for that matter—there is a dedicated segment of bowhunters who continue to build and use the most traditional bows and arrows. There are not many purist traditional archers, relatively speaking. But those who fit this description feel strongly about their sport. The best resource I have seen for how to build traditional bows and arrows is *The Traditional Bowyer's Bible*, published by Bois D'Arc Press (P.O. Box 233, Azle, TX 76020). This book thoroughly examines the steps in bow and arrow building, from cutting the tree to finishing the completed bow. It includes a chapter on arrow building and is a solid resource for the traditionalist.

Contributor to *The Traditional Bowyer's Bible*, Jay Massey, in his chapter "Why Traditional?" writes, "One of the primary benefits of using traditional archery gear—aside from saving lots of money, especially when you make your own gear—is that it promotes a sense of fun and encourages a carefree spirit. Archers who go traditional al-

Those bowhunters who enjoy "snap" shooting of upland game birds usually choose a long or recurve bow because they shoot instinctively and can come to full draw quickly.

Stringing a recurve takes a little practice, but is relatively simple when you know how. The proper method is being demonstrated here. When the bow is not in use, tension should be released.

ways seem to agree that once they make the switch, archery is once again exciting. Soon we are drawn into this ancient game and a simple stroll through the woods becomes an adventure in Sherwood Forest. For a moment, we are taken away from the complexities of a modern world and into a realm of mystery and romance. For a moment we have recaptured the spirit of traditional archery.''

"When I began shooting a bow in the 1940s, that's all there was—traditional equipment," says G. Fred Asbel, president of the Pope and Young Club. "I always thought bows were just gorgeous. When people came along with compound bows, they just didn't appeal to me. But then, again, I don't own a garage door opener and I don't like television."

Some people like Asbel began shooting traditional equipment and just never had a desire to switch to a compound. Other bowhunters, Asbel says, become traditional shooters after becoming proficient and successful with a compound. In a way, traditional bowhunting is analogous to fly fishing, he says. When someone starts fishing they probably purchase a rod and reel and some tackle. The next year they buy more lures designed to catch more and bigger fish. This continues, he says, until the fisherman has a large tackle box filled with lures and equipment designed to cast better and attract and catch more fish.

Eventually, Asbel says, some fishermen step out of the ''catch fish'' stage and get more into the technique of fishing. They still want to catch fish, but it's the technique's challenge that is exciting.

"When an angler starts fly fishing, he is usually not concerned about how many fish he catches," Asbel says. "He's concerned about the entire technique of fishing and fly presentation. It's the same thing with traditional archery. I find that a lot of traditional shooters spend 12 months a year being involved with a bow. But that doesn't make them better than people using modern equipment. Obviously, we know that some of the most effective hunters are shooting modern equipment. But there's room for everybody," Asbel says.

Basic Definitions
Traditional archers can shoot various bows—all in the "traditional" category. Here are the different types of traditional bows:

Longbow. A straight-end bow made in the style of the old English longbow. These bows are normally between 66 and 72 inches long.

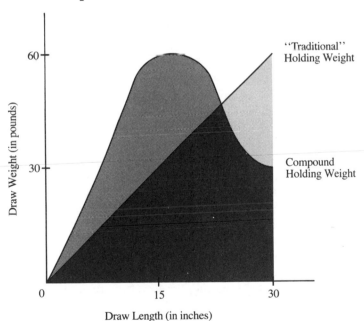

Comparison Of Force Draw Curves

A comparison of the force draw curves of a traditional bow and a compound points out the major differences between the two bows. A compound stores more potential energy with half the holding weight.

Longbows usually have narrow, thick limbs characterized by little or no drastic curvature in them.

Flatbow. Also a straight-limb bow, the flatbow resembles American Indian bows rather than English longbows. They are shorter than longbows and have wider, thinner limbs. This shorter design employed by Indians was easier to use on horseback. Modern flatbows usually range from 48 to 62 inches in length. Flatbows work well for hunting in heavy brush or from a tree stand.

Recurve. A recurve is nothing more than a longbow or flatbow with its ends permanently bent back away from the archer. In the Middle East and Asia, this bow has been used for thousands of years. Because of the reflexed limbs, recurve bows produce faster arrow speeds than longbows or flatbows, all else being equal. Recurve bows normally range from 56 to 64 inches in length.

Although the design hasn't changed much over the years, the materials used in some cases is very high-tech. The general result is that modern longbows shoot faster and smoother than earlier versions. This has attracted more converts to traditional-style shooting.

Equipment Selection And Performance

Traditional bows require an increasing draw force to bring them to full draw. A traditional shooter will hit peak draw weight at full draw. A compound shooter, by comparison, hits peak draw weight somewhere near the middle of the draw, then the draw "lets off" 50 or 65 percent, to 50 or 35 percent of peak draw weight. At full draw, a traditional archer shooting a 60-pound draw bow will hold 60 pounds. At full draw, a compound archer shooting a 60-pound draw bow will hold 21 or 30 pounds, depending upon let-off (65 or 50 percent respectively).

Despite the higher holding weight required with a recurve or longbow, a traditional bow stores less energy than a compound. The only energy available to the bow is the energy used to bring it to full draw. Energy expended to keep the bow at full draw does not increase the bow's stored energy—energy used to propel the arrow.

To understand the potential energy of a recurve or longbow, let's look at a draw force curve for such a bow. The shaded area represents the energy expended by the shooter to reach full draw. This is the only energy available to the bow. Now compare this to the stored energy of a modern compound bow. More stored energy, of course, translates into more potential arrow speed and, therefore, more potential kinetic energy.

Although a traditional bow will yield a slightly lower arrow speed

While expert bowhunters hunt dangerous big game such as a polar bear with a recurve bow, the major disadvantage is the difficulty in maintaining a full draw while waiting for the animal to assume the right position.

with less kinetic energy than a compound, the kinetic energy produced still makes it an efficient hunting tool capable of cleanly harvesting any North American big-game animal. Some, perhaps all, of bowhunting's most prominent early hunters shot traditional bows at one time, because that was the bow available. Fred Bear, for example, the man often credited with bringing this sport out of the Stone Age and into the Modern Age, used traditional equipment to harvest many big-game animals.

Although aluminum and carbon arrows are favored by many bowhunters, wood arrows are often used by traditionalists. The wood arrow is part of the challenge facing traditionalists: "I shoot wood arrows," says Asbel. "Currently, I'm testing some non-traditional wood, as well as using things that hunters have never used before. It gets me more involved in bowhunting—and that's what it's all about. I know that if I want to kill an animal with a bow and arrow I can. So I continue to challenge myself by trying different things yet not reducing the responsibility. I want to kill the animal cleanly."

Even though this sounds nostalgic and challenging, it can be a lot of work. Here's what Judd Cooney recalls about selecting and shooting wood-arrow shafts:

"When I made wooden shafts, I would buy 100 and spin them. Out of that 100 I would maybe get 12 to 20 that were halfway straight," he said. "Then, I would fletch and prepare them and go out and shoot, dividing them into groupings. I had some that shoot to the left, right, up and shoot down. So out of 100 shafts, I would maybe have 10 arrows that would shoot to the right and 10 arrows to the left. And the next day if the barometer changed, it all changed."

Instinctive Shooting

Most traditional bowhunters shoot instinctively—without sights. Even some compound shooters shoot without sights; it is a different proposition. "Shooting instinctively is just a basic skill that we all have," Asbel says. "Everyone who has fished or used a shotgun has been doing this entire instinctive thing and may have, in fact, walked right by it. However, with a bow and arrow, we think we need to make this really complex for some reason. Almost every single person has pointed his or her finger at something he or she was looking at. Instinctive shooting is nothing more than that, and traditional equipment somewhat falls right into that.

"Traditional equipment is so much simpler," he continues. "Once hunters try it and see that it is so much simpler, most of them really get involved. I'll take anybody with some degree of physical

Instinctive shooting and traditional bows seem to go hand-in-hand. Instinctive shooting, as demonstrated here, is a popular choice among "purists" who don't like to hang additional objects on the bow.

ability and after 30 minutes I'll have them shooting a doorknob at 10 yards at every shot. It has to do with starting with equipment that you can pull. Everybody has the ability to look at something and point their finger at it. That is so basic.

"Hunting with a bow and arrow is a very personal challenge," Asbel says. "Some people get into it with the intent of killing game. Typically, a person gets involved in bowhunting because it is a greater challenge. I think bowhunting is an evolutionary process. For example, the guy says, 'Last year I shot my first deer; this year I'm going to shoot my first buck.' And then maybe three years from now he will say, 'I want to shoot a Pope and Younger,' or he may say, 'I want to hunt with traditional equipment.' That is the sort of additional challenge I'm talking about. It's not so much the equipment as it is an indication of bowhunting evolution."

Technological improvements have been made in bows and bowhunting accessories. And yet, for some people, these accessories and improvements complicate or clutter a relatively simple sport. These are the people who prefer to shoot traditional equipment, who challenge not only their hunting instincts but also their shooting instincts.

The great thing about bowhunting is that the sport can accommodate a variety of participants—from the high-tech aficionado to the bare-bow traditionalist.

10

Working Toward A Silent Hunt

Select the best bow, the right arrow and the most effective broadhead. Outfit your rig with practical accessories. Tune your setup until you shoot perfectly through paper. Then pack up your gear and take it to the range on a calm, quiet morning. It should be just you, your bow and the target. Draw back. Aim carefully. Then do something different when you release. Instead of watching your arrow when you release, listen to the sound of your release. Do it again. Draw back. Aim. Shoot. Then listen. Every bow makes some noise when shot. Some bows will "thwap." Others will "zinngggg."

During a hunt, that sound will reach the game animal before your broadhead-tipped arrow does—that's inevitable. During that fraction of a second between the arrival of sound and the arrow, the animal can jump or duck or begin to flee. The result, as is occasionally heard, is an animal "jumping the string."

Even super-fast hunting bows can not deliver an arrow before the sound of your shot. To prevent a deer from jumping your string, you would need to increase your arrow speed to about 500 fps. That's impossible, however, because today's fastest hunting bows have arrow speeds from 250 to 270 fps.

This means an arrow fired from your bow at 250 fps (roughly one-fourth the speed of sound) will reach a deer 30 yards away in .36 second. However, the sound of the arrow's release will reach the deer in .08 second, leaving about .25 second or so for the deer to react. Researchers say that deer can react to an outside stimulus in .10 second or less. This gives the deer more than enough time to "jump the string."

However, if you could double the speed of your arrow to 500 fps, you would cut the time it takes the arrow to reach the deer in half (.18 second). Then, the arrow would arrive in the same amount of time that it would normally take for the deer to hear the shot and react to it. That doesn't appear to be possible.

It simply is not possible with current technology to accurately shoot a broadhead-tipped arrow 500 fps at a target 30 yards away. Game, therefore, probably always will be able to hear the sound of the arrow's release before it reaches the target. And game, therefore, will always have the opportunity to flinch or move or jump. A bowhunter might as well accept that fact and move on in his quest to quiet his hunt.

Silence Your Arrow Rest

Bowhunters can't control the speed of sound, but they can control how much noise their bows make at the release. And they can, to some degree, release their shots when the animals are less tense and less likely to jump the string.

Well-known bowhunter Bob Fratzke says the most common mistake bowhunters make is having a noisy setup. Fratzke, who has harvested more than 24 trophy-class whitetails, says that a noisy arrow rest is the most common source of bow noise.

"Bowhunters can have the best equipment," Fratzke says. "They can practice and shoot very well, but the most common thing they forget when they're bowhunting is to silence their arrow rests. Think about it. A whitetail walks by within bow range and a bowhunter will have this bright, shiny rest. When he draws the arrow, it is pulled across that rest and goes 'shhhwoo.' That sound has got these deer already trying to get out of the way before the hunter releases his shot. That's probably the biggest mistake bowhunters can make."

And even more game-spooking noise is made when a bowhunter's arrow travels over that unprotected rest, Fratzke says.

Teflon, rubber tubing or moleskin placed on all exposed parts will quiet rests. However, always carry extra tubing and moleskin; teflon and rubber tubing will wear down with use, exposing the metal rest again. Moleskin, for example, can peel off with a single shot or simply wear through with normal use. If you shoot a shoot-around rest, you should attach a small patch of moleskin to the cushion plunger. It's also good to attach two extra moleskin strips and two

Moleskin can be a big help in silencing your equipment. As indicated, moleskin should be applied to the arrow rest, the arrow shelf, sight window and to the bottom of the pin protector to reduce the sound of arrow contact.

A penetrating lubricant such as WD-40 or Bohning's Sportlube "B" can quiet the groaning axles sometimes found on new bows. Apply the lubricant and pull the bowstring back partway several times to work it in.

moleskin patches to your sight window. Then, if one or the other slips off the rest during a hunt, it's a simple matter to peel the moleskin off the sight window and attach the skin to the plunger or rest. This is an inexpensive way to save a back-country hunt.

Protect The Sight Window

Even though you are extremely careful, a nocked arrow will occasionally slip off the rest and hit the sight window or bow handle. That sound can alert and spook nearby game. Placing moleskin on the arrow shelf below the rest will greatly reduce or eliminate this kind of noise. Also, attach moleskin to places where a nocked arrow could touch the bow handle.

Bowhunters on extended hunts should always carry extra moleskin, as well as a small bottle of powdered graphite for in-the-field bow silencing. Including these items in a small tackle box that will fit in your day pack can be a hunt saver.

Lubricating Bow Axles, Cables And Wheels

Penetrating spray lubricants, which can be purchased at any hardware store, can work wonders on a groaning axle. Simply apply the spray and let it sit for a short time. Then draw back and let down your bow several times, working the lubricant into the axles. Repeat this process, then wipe off any excess lubricant on the wheels, limbs and axles. One application will usually last the season. However, on back-country hunts, it's best to carry a small can of penetrating lubricant—just in case. During such hunts, you should draw back often to ensure your bow is still silent. Sometimes, rain and heavy use can wear away the penetrating lubricant.

One of my favorite, most accurate bows had a serious problem when I first got it. The top eccentric would "screech" whenever the bow was pulled back to full draw. According to the manufacturer, the noise was probably caused by the cable as it spooled out of the eccentric's cable channel.

Powdered graphite works well in hushing the squeak or groan of cables and eccentrics. Apply a line of graphite on the cable channel and then draw the bow several times to work it into the channel. You may have to do it again if the bow gets wet.

A bow stabilizer like this Saunders Torque Tamer quiets your bow by absorbing bow energy after the shot. Stabilizers can also help to tighten your groups.

The problem was easily solved by working a line of powdered graphite into the cable channel by drawing and then letting down several times. More powdered graphite was applied into the cable channels while the bow was held at full draw. (This, of course, was a two-person job.) That took care of the problem, but I still apply powdered graphite occasionally to the cable channels, especially if I've been hunting in wet conditions.

The manufacturer of that bow reports that new eccentrics sometimes have a sharp edge on the cable groove that does not precisely fit the cable. That's the reason for the screeching. Shooting while allowing the eccentrics' cable grooves and cables to ''marry'' should also reduce this kind of bow noise.

Shoot With A Bow Stabilizer

Bow stabilizers help quiet a hunting bow by absorbing some of the energy that is transferred to the bow when the arrow is released. When the bowstring is released, much of the bow's stored energy is transferred to the arrow. However, not all the energy is transferred —especially if the archer is shooting light arrow shafts. That energy ends up coursing through the bow and rattling the accessories. Much of this energy can be absorbed by a stabilizer.

The only time you might not use a bow stabilizer is when its weight is of paramount concern. A bowhunt high into the mountains for goats or sheep, for example, might prompt you to consider leaving the bow stabilizer at home. Personally, it would have to be an extremely physically-taxing hunt before I would leave behind a 9½-ounce device that noticeably quiets a bow. The added measure of confidence the stabilizer provides is worth the additional weight.

Apply Graphite To The Cable Guard

A cable guard holds tightly strung cable away from the arrow shaft. Most often, a plastic cable guard slide is used to protect the cables from the metal cable guard. This tiny cable guard slide withstands extraordinary friction. When the bowstring is released, that slide moves across the metal cable guard, and the cables slip through the cable-guard slide with lightning speed. The activity and the resulting intense friction can translate into bow noise during the release.

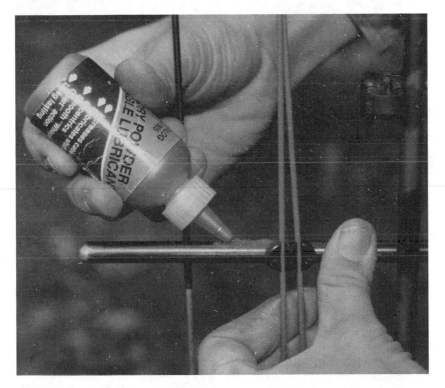

The cable guard slide can be a big bow noise-producer. Quiet the noise by applying powdered graphite as shown between the cable guard and the slide.

String silencers are another means of quieting bow noise. Whether you prefer the rubber cat whiskers (left) or the yarn-like puff balls, string silencers have been found to reduce bowstring vibrations by up to 74 percent.

To quiet a cable-guard slide, apply a line of powdered graphite between the cable guard and the cable guard slide. To spread the graphite, simply draw back and let down. Occasionally, you may need to make an additional application of graphite, especially when you're hunting in wet conditions. During extended hunts, always carry a small tube of powdered graphite.

Attach String Silencers
One sure-fire way to reduce bow noise is to install string silencers at least 6 inches from each axle. Both rubber cat whiskers and yarn-like puff balls are inexpensive, easy to install and effective.

Select A Quiet Bow
Because of their design, some bows are quieter than others.
"The most important consideration for me is that a bow be functionally quiet," says Myles Keller, "not only when you release an

arrow, but also when you draw.'' Keller has taken nine whitetails in the past seven years with the Xi Legend bow.

Designing a quiet bow was a primary concern for Chuck Adams and technical experts at Hoyt who set out to design the Hoyt Super Slam bow. ''The Super Slam is a very quiet bow,'' says Chuck, ''partly because we designed the handle riser with no vibration focal points. Everything on the handle riser is a nice easy curve, and there's no sharp edges or dramatic changes in metal direction. That means vibrations flow smoothly through the handle riser to the stabilizer-hole area. If you've got a stabilizer on your bow, the vibrations don't turn into noise in the handle riser; they just flow right out the front. If you have a proper stabilizer, it vibrates and disperses that energy without a lot of noise.

''Also,'' Adams says, ''the cable guard is offset and shorter compared to other bows. A shorter cable guard requires less aluminum, and that means less material for vibrations to flow through and cause noise.''

Select Soft, Quiet Clothes

Bowhunters trying to attain a silent hunt must also consider their clothing. No matter what type of camouflage pattern you select, it must be made of a fabric which allows you to draw your bow without a sound. Lots of fabrics—including wool, cotton and fleece—are exceptionally quiet.

When selecting your hunting outfit, put on the shirt or coat and go to a quiet corner of the store. Then, go through the motions of drawing your bow. Listen. Stand up and sit down. Does the outfit make any sound as you draw? Does the zipper bounce? Does the lining in the arm crinkle as you pretend to draw back? If you can hear your clothes in a retail store, chances are a game animal will hear that sound in the field. Select clothes which are comfortable—and quiet.

Until recently, bowhunters who wanted to hunt in wet weather and stay dry had to give up a degree of quietness. Waterproof fabrics were often treated with a rubber coating that resulted in game-spooking noise at nearly every movement. Today, however, there's a bevy of quiet, waterproof camouflage garments for bowhunters. Visit your local pro shop or sporting goods store for a complete selection.

Change Your Hunting Style

Another way to keep a deer from jumping the string is to take the shot when the animal is relaxed. An alert deer—one expecting danger—is much more apt to jump the string than a deer quietly browsing or moving slowly along the trail. Therefore, look for a hunting location where the deer might feel secure and be more relaxed. Often game will relax once they're inside thick cover. In the transition zone between open country and protective cover, game will often slow down and proceed with caution.

Once a deer has come within range, wait until it relaxes before you release your shot. Waiting for its head to go down or its suspicions to subside will lessen the chance of the animal "jumping the string."

Another consideration is wind direction. If you are conscious about scent, you probably selected a stand which is downwind from the trail. This wind can also help carry these sounds away from the animal.

The sound of the shot will reach the game animal before the broadhead-tipped arrow does. That is inevitable. All you can do is silence your setup as much as possible and alter hunting style to shoot at relaxed game.

11

Tips For Increasing Arrow Speed

Bowhunters have one truth they can invest in: A fast arrow has two significant advantages over a slow arrow, all else being equal. First, a fast arrow has a flatter trajectory which compensates for range-estimation errors. Second, the faster arrow also has more kinetic energy. Kinetic energy, of course, is the leading factor in determining penetration potential. These are the two major reasons why bowhunters and bow manufacturers have so aggressively pursued obtaining faster arrow velocities.

To compare the velocities of compound bows, the Archery Manufacturers Organization (AMO) established industry standards: The bow must have a 60-pound draw weight and 30-inch draw length and the arrow must weigh 540 grains. Thus, when you see the report of an arrow speed of 235 fps based on AMO standards, you know that the bow was set up with a 60-pound draw weight and 30-inch draw length and was shooting a 540-grain arrow.

During the past 25 years, technology has taken bows and bowhunting accessories to new levels—from machined handles to computer-designed eccentrics to carbon arrows. With this technology, arrow velocities have increased by about 15 percent. On average, a recurve produces an arrow speed of 205 fps; a wheel-operated compound produces an arrow speed of 210 fps; and a cam-operated compound produces an arrow speed of 235 fps. Ignoring the improvements in consistency, technological advancements during those 25 years have boosted arrow speeds by up to 30 fps.

Your setup may vary from these average arrow speeds. However, chances are good that there are tactics you can use and equipment you can install to boost your bow's arrow velocity.

For the purpose of illustrating this, let's create a speed-seeking bowhunter who shoots a cam-operated compound producing an arrow velocity of 235 fps. By how much can he increase the arrow speed of his setup? Some of the fastest hunting bows on the market boast an AMO arrow speed of 250 fps. Can his arrow speed approach that speed? (Here's a tickler: If our mythical bowhunter implements the five changes described here, he will boost his arrow speed higher than 250 fps.) Here, then, are five steps to boost a bow's performance.

Increase Draw Weight

The most effective technique for increasing arrow speed is to put more energy into drawing the bow. The more energy expended in drawing the bow, the more energy available for the bow to use. It's that simple. One option, then, is to increase the bow's peak draw weight.

For every pound of increase in peak draw weight, there should be a 1.4- to 1.8-fps arrow-velocity increase. Assume the imaginary bowhunter increases his draw weight by 10 pounds from 60 to 70 pounds. By doing so, he will increase his arrow velocity by 14 to 18 fps. Choosing the low number (14) means arrow speed should increase from 235 fps to 249 fps—nearing the performance level, according to AMO standards, of today's top production bows. However, an increase in draw weight may also require an increase in the spine stiffness of the arrow shafts. (Consult arrow shaft selection charts to determine how much you can increase draw weight before increasing your arrow shafts' spine.)

Reduce Total Arrow Weight

Arrow velocity also can be increased by reducing total arrow weight. The lighter the projectile, the faster it will fly out of the bow, all else being equal. Total arrow weight can be reduced either by shooting a lighter broadhead or a lighter arrow shaft.

It is generally believed that for every nine grains of total arrow weight reduction, arrow velocity will increase by one foot per second. Perhaps our bowhunter can reduce his broadhead weight from 125 grains to 110 grains while still keeping the 7 to 10 percent weight-forward ratio discussed in Chapter 6. This 15-grain reduction, then,

Arrow velocity can be determined by shooting the arrow through a chronograph. The machine clocks the speed of the arrow and provides a digital readout.

will increase arrow velocity by 1.7 fps. Those first two steps alone will boost the arrow speed of this "average" cam-operated compound to 250.7 fps.

To reduce actual arrow weight, shoot lighter shafts of the same length or shoot shorter shafts. Assume the bowhunter is shooting 2317s that weigh 411 grains—based on the size recommendation from the Easton Hunting Shaft Selection Chart. For starters, he could shoot 2514s, which weigh 351 grains—reducing arrow weight by 60 grains. This 60-grain reduction would increase arrow speed by 6.6 fps to 256.3 fps.

To further increase speed, attach an overdraw system that shortens total arrow length from 1 to 5 inches. Cutting just 2 inches from a 2514 will reduce arrow weight by an additional 22 grains (down to 329 grains) and, subsequently, boost arrow velocity by an additional 2.4 fps. Total arrow speed now climbs to 258.7 fps!

There is a danger, however, in going to shafts which are too light for this hunting setup. AMO issued a warning regarding total arrow weight amid the never-ending pursuit for speed: The total arrow weight should be no less than 6 grains per pound of peak draw weight. The reason for this warning is some bowhunters and 3-D shooters were shooting extremely light shafts that did not absorb all of the bow's stored energy. Although arrow speeds were blistering, leftover energy was absorbed by the bows, resulting in shattered limbs. With a mythical setup geared to 70 pounds, total arrow weight must add up to at least 420 grains. In this setup, the arrow weight would be 110 grains (broadhead) + 329 grains (arrow shaft) + 35 grains (fletching plus nock) = 474 grains. That's well above the 420-grain minimum established by AMO.

Shoot A Fast-Flight String

Fast-Flight bowstrings weigh less than conventional Dacron strings. The reduced weight results in increased arrow speed, because a lighter string moves faster than a heavier string. If your bow has a Dacron bowstring, consider exchanging it for a Fast-Flight string which should increase arrow velocity, on average, by six fps.

The mythical bowhunter who shoots 235 fps, most likely has a Fast-Flight string on his bow. Even though this is an option, assume the hunter is already shooting a Fast-Flight string.

Shoot Cams Rather Than Wheels

Most modern bows are available with cams or round wheels. All else being equal, cams will generate up to 15 fps more arrow velocity.

If the bows are properly tuned and the same weight arrow is used in each of these bows, the cam-operated bow (right) should produce an arrow speed up to 15 fps faster than the round-wheel bow.

Our mythical bowhunter, of course, is already shooting a cam-operated compound so we can't include this potential 15 fps increase. (The advantages and disadvantages of cams were discussed in Chapter 3.

Lower Let-Off

Although let-off allows shooters to stay at full draw longer, there is a price that is paid—although not a big one. That price is expressed in arrow velocity. For every 13 percent increase in holding weight, there is a 3- to 5-fps increase in arrow velocity. For instance, if this hunter were shooting a 65 percent let-off bow that produced 258.7 fps arrow speed, he could increase arrow speed by at least 3 fps to 261.7 fps by stepping down to 50 percent let-off. Of course, he would have to make the decision whether the increase in holding weight from 24.5 to 36.4 pounds (50 versus 65 percent let-off) is worth this 3-fps increase in arrow velocity.

He could achieve the same arrow-speed increase by boosting peak draw weight (currently at 70 pounds) by 3 pounds. That 3-pound increase in draw weight would translate to a one pound increase in holding weight, based upon his 65 percent let-off. Then, instead of holding 35.4 pounds (at 50 percent let-off and 70-pound draw), he would hold just 25.5 pounds (at 65 percent let-off and 73-

pound draw). That would seem to be the better approach.

These are techniques bowhunters can use to boost arrow velocity. They won't work for every bowhunter. Some experienced bowhunters rightly promote the adage to "keep it simple," while many others pursue the tantalizing goal of more and more arrow speed. These techniques can help you achieve greater arrow speed without abusing your equipment.

The mythical bowhunter could have a setup—although no longer at AMO standards but above the 6-grain minimum—that shoots arrows at 261.7 fps. Originally, his bow was shooting at 235 fps. He could have increased his arrow speed by 11.4 percent. (That's significant, especially when a round-wheel compound only increased arrow velocity by 2.4 percent over a recurve.) And, cam-operated bows featuring the latest technological advancements increased arrow velocity by 14.6 percent over a recurve and 12.2 percent over a round-wheel compound.

A Warning About Arrow Speed

Bowhunters should be warned, however, that the side effects of blazing arrow speeds are not always enjoyable. A fast bow is less forgiving and noisier. You may also have to shoot a mechanical release aid to get the clean release required for that kind of speed.

"A highly tuned, precision bow—one with an overdraw and the cams and everything on it—is like driving a Ferrari hunting," says Judd Cooney. "As long as everything is just right, you get by fine. But if you encounter muddy roads and rocks—less than ideal conditions—not only may you be less efficient, but you could be done altogether."

12

Crossbows For Disabled Hunters

A ccidents happen. More than a decade ago, a car crash left Marvin Vought a quadriplegic. Before the accident, Vought of New Alexandria, Pennsylvania, was a bowhunter; after the accident, he couldn't draw his bow. "I tried shooting my hand-held bow six or seven times," Vought recalls, "but there was no way I could pull it back."

Today, thanks to Vought's determination and the Pennsylvania Game Commission's special crossbow permit for disabled hunters, Marvin Vought can once again bowhunt white-tailed deer. Pennsylvania, like more than a dozen other states, allows the use of crossbows by physically disabled hunters during the regular archery deer season.

Most NAHC Members can draw back a compound or traditional bow, and do it without thinking—like walking up a flight of stairs or turning a page in this book; however, there are NAHC Members who do not have the physical abilities of others. For those hunters, using a crossbow during the archery deer season may be the only opportunity they have to hunt big game, particularly during relatively mild weather conditions.

"Hunting with a crossbow gives disabled hunters a terrific sense of independence and accomplishment," says Vought, who is vice president of Pennsylvania Sportsmen For The Disabled (Rd. 1, Box 470, New Alexandria, PA 15670). "Just to get out there and hunt with a crossbow is the biggest thrill of their life," he continues. "Most quads have a self-cocking crossbow. And hunting during the archery deer season gets them into the woods during a better time of the year when there are fewer people and the weather is generally better than during the gun season."

In Pennsylvania, physically disabled hunters can use a crossbow during the archery deer season. In addition to rules pertaining to this special crossbow permit, all other archery regulations apply.

"From a disabled person's perspective, the advantage of a crossbow is that the bow can be held in the cocked position," explains David Sullivan, founder and president of Alabama Handicapped Sportsmen. Sullivan said many physically disabled hunters do not have the ability to draw back a hand-held bow and hold it at full draw.

As president of the Alabama Handicapped Sportsmen (44 Huntington Place, Northport AL, 35476), Sullivan was one of the major forces behind an Alabama law passed in 1991 that permits disabled hunters to use crossbows during the state's archery deer season. Sullivan, who was injured in a car-motorcycle accident in the mid-1970s, leads a group of about 140 disabled hunters; thus, he doesn't expect a sudden surge in the number of requests for Alabama crossbow permits. However, he does expect it (the special permit) to open up new hunting opportunities for a small group of disabled hunters.

To obtain a crossbow permit in Alabama, a hunter must request an application from the state's Department of Conservation and Natural Resources. A state-licensed doctor must examine the hunter to determine if the applicant is physically disabled according to state guidelines. Then the doctor and applicant must sign the application and have it notarized. The Department of Conservation and Natural Resources determines whether the applicant should receive a permit to hunt with a crossbow during the archery deer season. Disabled hunters who receive the permit must buy the annual archery deer tag.

Pennsylvania, in addition to having the application signed by a doctor, requires the hunter to be interviewed by a state game warden before the permit is issued.

Alberta province, which authorized use of crossbows by disabled hunters in 1991, also requires a letter from a doctor. The province not only gave disabled hunters the opportunity to hunt with a crossbow but also relaxed rules governing off-road vehicle use in hunting by disabled hunters.

Crossbow Mechanics And Nomenclature

Basically, the advantage of a crossbow is it mechanically holds

The crossbow has provided an opportunity for many disabled bowhunters to get back into the field and pursue their love of hunting, as well as experience scenes like this.

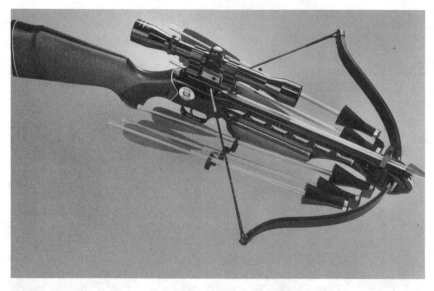

At first glance, a crossbow looks like a hybrid between a firearm and a bow and arrow. However, its arrow speed and kinetic energy make it very similar to a hand-held compound bow.

the bowstring at full draw. Most hunting crossbows have a 100- to 150-pound draw weight and a self-cocking mechanism. This is ideal for disabled hunters.

The hunter aims the crossbow much the same way he would aim a rifle or shotgun—one hand on the forend, the other on the pistol grip, cheek down on the stock and shoulder into the butt. The shooter aims using open bow sights or a low-powered scope.

A trigger releases the string. As the string travels forward, it propels a short arrow shaft (or bolt) which typically is at least 14 inches long. Many states require crossbow hunters to shoot a broadhead weighing at least 100 grains.

Despite the heavy draw weight and short arrow shaft, a crossbow does not produce exceptional trajectory. Many crossbow manufacturers encourage hunters to take shots within 20 yards. Research conducted by Horton Manufacturing, a major crossbow manufacturer, found the trajectories of arrows fired from a 60-pound compound and a 150-pound crossbow to be very similar. Sullivan says he limits himself to shots under 20 yards. This is because an arrow shot from his crossbow drops 18 inches in 40 yards. Like a hand-held bow, a crossbow kills by causing hemorrhaging.

Complete crossbow packages sold by some manufacturers contain everything a first-time shooter needs to get started. A typical out-fit might include a 125- or 150-pound, draw-weight crossbow, standard pin sight, bow-mounted arrow quiver and properly spined bolts. According to figures released by manufacturers, this type of setup could produce an arrow speed of 223 fps and 45.3 foot-pounds of energy; maximum hunting range for this setup would be 30 yards.

Horton Stops Dryfire Problem

For years, compound-crossbow owners have risked damage to their crossbows' cables, limbs or wheels when dryfiring or shooting without an arrow mounted on the string. A tremendous amount of energy is generated in the short power stroke of a 150-pound-pull compound crossbow. Dryfire damage is seldom covered by manufacturer's warranty. During the firing of a crossbow, both the string and the arrow absorb a great amount of energy. If there is no arrow, all that energy is concentrated in the compound configuration of limbs, cable, cable teardrops and wheels.

To eliminate the potential for a damaging dryfire, Horton introduced an innovative No-Dryfire mechanism. The mechanism is standard on Horton crossbows. When the crossbow is cocked, the safety is automatically engaged. The safety on models with the No-Dryfire

When a Horton crossbow is cocked, the safety is automatically engaged. Horton's No-Dryfire mechanism cannot be moved to the "fire" position until the arrow is snugly seated.

mechanism cannot be moved to the ''fire'' position unless an arrow is snugly seated against the string.

Recognition Of Crossbow Seasons

Thirty-six states and six Canadian provinces recognize the crossbow as a legal hunting weapon in some way, according to a survey by a crossbow maker, Horton Manufacturing. ''There are 18 states,'' Horton reports, ''which permit the physically disabled—usually with some form of physician's certification—to utilize a crossbow during the archery season.

''In states like Arkansas, Ohio and Kentucky where very limited crossbow seasons were established at the beginning,'' Horton says, ''state officials—seeing little impact on harvest totals as a result— have opted for extending the opportunity for those wishing to utilize the crossbow.'' According to Horton, no established crossbow season has been shortened or discontinued because of over-harvest, illegal taking of game with a crossbow or crossbow hunting accidents.

''The crossbow has been used for deer hunting in Ohio since 1976,'' said Clayton Lakes, chief of the Ohio Department of Natural Resources. ''We have found the crossbow to be an effective deer-hunting implement when used within its capabilities.'' The crossbow season in Ohio runs concurrently with the state's longbow season.

13

Proven Practice Techniques

Remember Bob Atwill from Chapter 1? When Bob settled the pin on the bull's vitals and released the arrow, he was at one of life's most exciting crossroads. If his shot was accurate, that satisfying moment would live with him for the rest of his life. Unfortunately, he missed. And that moment, as well, will live with him. Few other sports have such infrequent opportunities for success. Of course, that added challenge is why many of us bowhunt.

Every bowhunter invests considerable time and money for perhaps one, or maybe two, shot opportunities per year. When asked, every bowhunter says that he or she practices. There is no reason not to believe it. Bob Atwill practiced. He told us about his Wednesday night and Saturday morning practice sessions. Yet, sometimes other bowhunters like Bob miss those once-in-a-year, or perhaps once-in-a-lifetime, shots. Why?

"That's why they call it hunting, not shooting," an ardent bowhunter responds when asked this question.

True. But still it can be downright difficult to return from a $3,000 hunt empty-handed. Is there a solution?

Getting Some Answers

In an attempt to find some answers, some of North America's most successful bowhunters were asked this question: "What practice strategies do you use to get into top shooting form?" Here are the responses, some of which may surprise you, from these bowhunters.

"Accuracy under any condition starts with good shooting form," says 20-year bowhunting veteran Dwight Schuh. "A lot of people may not agree with this, but I practice form a lot. I think it is very valuable to work on shooting form and get the basic form down solid. Then you have a fundamental system. I spend perhaps 80 percent of my time practicing good shooting form. Then, when I get into an awkward position or a strange environment or when I am fatigued, good shooting form is ingrained in me so much that I'm going to shoot correctly."

If you spend all your time practicing awkward shooting situations, Schuh says, you may never develop a good shooting form.

For Schuh, practicing good shooting form continues even during the hunt. "I have an eight-arrow quiver on my bow and two of my arrows have rubber blunts," he says. "I shoot constantly when I'm hunting. If I take a break for lunch or if I'm just walking down the trail, I'm always pulling arrows off my bow and taking a shot. If I see a rotten stump or a pine cone, I take a shot. I think this constant practice under real hunting conditions is very beneficial because I'm tired or cold. These are the same conditions under which I will have to take a shot if an elk suddenly appears.

"That's the most valuable practice I have," he continues. "I think it's a real mistake to put eight broadheads into your bow quiver and then go into the field for a week without taking a practice shot. You're just not going to be ready when the time comes."

Schuh says he learned good shooting form from fellow bowhunters and top competitive archers, including an Olympic archery coach, professional archery instructor and a professional archer.

Chuck Adams, a recognized outstanding bowhunter, recommends practicing at least three months before the season begins.

"Ease into the whole process," he says, "and stop as soon as you get tired." Chuck advises against flinging arrows frantically just two or three weeks before the season, because "that can thoroughly whip your body. It's also a common way to develop bad shooting habits. It's better to shoot fewer arrows deliberately, and learn from each shot."

Despite his status as possibly the world's most successful bowhunter, Chuck still practices shooting five hours a week. His most common practice strategy is to wait 30 seconds to one minute between shots. He says this gives him the opportunity to concentrate on shooting form and time to analyze and understand what he is doing right or wrong.

This bowhunter is using an animal target, making his practice session more realistic. He's memorizing the image of the ''deer's'' vitals so he will have no adjustments to make in the field.

"Sometimes I may take more time if I have a shooting problem and I'm trying to figure out what I'm doing wrong," he explains. "But it has been my experience that you are better off to take a shot, and then analyze your basic shooting form. If the arrow went in the right place, try to figure out what you did right; if it went in the wrong place, think about what you did wrong.

"The other recommendation, and it's something that I adhere to religiously," he says, "is don't shoot every day. Serious weight lifters work out no more than every other day to give their muscles the opportunity to repair and rebuild. Archers should do the same thing. You'll never catch a good tournament archer shooting the day before a tournament. If you shoot every day, especially with higher-draw-weight hunting equipment, you're breaking down your muscles and not allowing them to mend between practice sessions."

Adams and Schuh agree that proper shooting form is critical. Adams says he learned to shoot by trial and error because there were no good step-by-step instructions available on proper shooting form. "I learned some very bad habits that I had to break over the years," Adams says. "It's a lot easier to develop good habits to begin with." Adams learned during this trial-and-error period that there are six steps to a solid shooting form.

Steps To Good Shooting

Stance. The average bowhunter should use a slightly open stance with toes pointed slightly toward the target. This does a couple things in helping the shooter. First, it shortens the draw length an inch or two. It's usually easier to get good arrow flight with a shorter arrow. Second, facing the target slightly moves the bowstring and its path away from the bowhunter's chest and bow arm. If the string even slightly touches either place, the shooter will experience wild arrow flight to the side. That wild arrow flight will be amplified when broadheads are being used.

Draw. A bowhunter shouldn't raise the bow high in the air and then draw by pushing with one arm and pulling with the other. Instead, extend the bow arm toward the target and draw the string straight back to your anchor. This is better because it's easier on the body, and there is less game-spooking motion.

Anchor. A solid anchor is crucial. It corresponds to the rear sight of a rifle. Finger shooters and bowhunters who prefer release aids must establish a consistent, comfortable anchor. A consistent anchor does not happen by accident; it is something good shooters think about and work at developing.

The author demonstrates the proper stance and positioning when using a mechanical release in shooting. Develop a set pattern for getting into position so that you can eliminate as many variables as possible.

Aim. Whatever aiming method you use, be consistent. Either come down on a target or up on a target or onto a target from left to right or right to left. Focusing on the sight pins or the target is a subject of some debate. Some archers concentrate on the sight pins while others concentrate on the target. Do one or the other; but, don't focus between the two points. Chuck Adams prefers to focus on the target. "In hunting situations I want my attention on the animal," he says. "Shooting targets on the range is another deal, but for hunting I think it's best to focus on the target.

"However, some people with buck fever focus on the sight pins and throw the animal out of focus," he adds. "That detaches them from the animal and makes them less nervous."

Release. If a bowhunter does not have a slick, consistent bowstring release, he can never expect to be accurate. Release-aid shooters should avoid punching the trigger or the release button the way some shotgun hunters slap the trigger. A finger shooter should always concentrate on a clean release, learning to keep the hand alongside the face, rather than plucking the string and throwing the hand out from the face.

Follow-through. Bowhunters using sights should keep the chosen sight pin on the target until the arrow actually hits. Of course, no shooter can keep it exactly on the target because the bow will always recoil. However, in consciously trying to keep the sight on the target, the shooter shouldn't do anything dramatically wrong before the arrow actually leaves the bow. Otherwise, the shooter will drop the bow or throw the bow to one side as the arrow is propelled forward. That always ruins accuracy.

Mental And Physical Preparation

Your practices, of course, should also include mental practice sessions. Before stepping into the woods, prepare yourself mentally for the shot. Also, decide in advance what size animal you will shoot. If you are taking any legal animal, all you need to do is get ready for the shot.

During an October deer hunt, for example, the temperature was below zero with a wind chill between 30 and 40 degrees below zero. While walking to my tree stand that first morning, I soon decided I would take any buck or doe, but not a fawn. That first day was long and miserable. After sitting for three hours, 15 feet high in a tree in the cold, I discovered that you can get cold even if you're outfitted with every article of clothing you own. I had four layers on my head, six layers on my torso, and four layers on my legs. Encumbered with these clothes and being out in these conditions lowered my standards. It didn't have to be a 6-point or better buck. Harvesting a deer under these adverse conditions—regardless of its rack size or gender, I decided—would make it a respectable deer.

During the afternoon of the second day, a deer worked its way down the trail toward me. I couldn't tell for sure at first whether it was a buck or a doe, but it was not a fawn. As the deer worked its way down the trail, I slowly pulled my hands from my pockets, took the bow off the hook, stood, positioned myself and held my bow at the ready. It was a doe. In a simple, quiet move, I drew my bow and aimed. The pin settled perfectly behind the doe's front shoulder as she passed broadside 12 yards from my stand.

In theory, at least, every bowhunter should assume he or she will shoot if a game animal is encountered and get into a shooting position as soon as possible. That way the hunter will be prepared for the shot-—whether it is taken or not. Human nature, however, being what it is, makes hunters unpredictable. For example, if I'm hunting for a buck and I see a deer, I immediately want to know whether it's a buck or a doe. If it's a buck, I want to know how big—whether it has six, eight or 10 points. I would look for answers to these questions; then I would get into position. Sometimes, I wish I had the discipline to get into position first and wait to determine the size of the animal until just before the shot. But the desire to determine the animal's size is, perhaps, inseparable from the predatory instinct. I'd like to believe an owl or hawk has some heightened sense of enthusiasm as it dives for a mature, full-grown snowshoe rather than a hapless, month-old, recently weaned bunny.

Being mentally prepared also means being ready to take the shot immediately when the opportunity presents itself. I'll never forget how unprepared I was during my first pronghorn bowhunt out West. I was hunting with Mel Dutton, inventor of the Mel Dutton Pronghorn Decoy. On the first morning of the hunt, just as we had set up the decoy, the very first pronghorn buck we spotted came right to us just as Mel had predicted. About 30 yards in front of us, the buck turned and walked broadside, parallel to the decoy. I rose to my knees and drew my bow. That movement startled and froze the buck and he stared right at me. My pin was already behind his front shoulder; that moment—that sliver of time that I had in which to shoot—was perhaps only a second or two. I heard Mel whisper "Now" in a hushed voice that disappeared with the wind through the prairie grass. But as Mel's encouragement registered, the buck turned and trotted away. Mel, I remember, shook his head, looked down at the grass and

Bowhunter Myles Keller prefers practicing alone. Most of his practice sessions involve shooting from his tree stand at a 3-D target in the woods. This prepares him more for the shot he will need to make to get his trophy.

smiled. I had not prepared myself that morning to draw, aim and shoot at the first opportunity. (Later, as the decoy continued its work, I harvested a respectable pronghorn.)

Mental preparation seems to be a problem for most first-year bowhunters. It becomes second nature, except in my case, for experienced bowhunters to be mentally prepared. At least, that's what they say!

My favorite mental-practice strategy is to imagine myself drawing, aiming and shooting. I'll often do this as I'm driving to the hunt area or hiking to my stand. Sometimes, even in my tree stand, I'll imagine getting ready for the shot, drawing silently, aiming and releasing. "Remember form," I tell myself. "Relax, release clean."

A practice strategy that combines both mental and physical practice is used by Myles Keller, senior pro-staff shooter with Indian Industries, Xi bows and accessories manufacturer. "Everybody is different," Keller says, "but I don't get a lot out of going to the target range with a bunch of people. That's basically exercise for me.

"What I like to do is to go into the woods by myself and set up 3-D, life-size targets and my tree stand," he continues. "I sit in my stand and imagine that I'm hunting and that this is the real thing. I try to apply the pressure to each shot. Using this technique I can get myself mentally prepared a lot better than I can through field practice. When I'm practicing with other people, we're usually just shooting for fun. I think there's a lot of people who can get something out of that type of group practice, but I can't. I want to be able to envision the shot, and I can only do that by myself."

Keller says he will look away from the target and then look back at it and think, "Okay, let's take the shot now."

Keller, who has been bowhunting for 30 years, says that experienced bowhunters begin to remember good shooting form with a little practice. "For people who have been shooting for many years, and have good shooting form, what presents a continual challenge is judging distance," he said. "Judging distance is something I can practice almost anywhere. If I'm in a store, I'll estimate how far it is to something, then pace it off. When I'm outside, I'll guess how far away something is, and then pace it off."

Target practice, although not for everyone, provides bowhunters with one of the easiest and best ways to become familiar with and tune their hunting setups. In fact, in metropolitan areas, target shooting can be the most common—even the only—practice opportunity for bowhunters.

"Whether I'm shooting at a target or a hunting setup, I like to get a small aiming dot and practice nothing more than good aim, good follow-through and good release," says three-time world archery champion and four-time National Field Archery Association champion Terry Ragsdale. "I like to practice and tune my setup at the longer ranges because then I'll have a good setup at any distance. A lot of times you can have a setup that appears to group extremely well up close, but the farther back you get, the worse it may group.

"Whether I am getting ready for a tournament or a hunt," he continues, "my main goal is to understand how a bow is grouping. I don't have a predetermined practice strategy when I go out to do that. I generally try to find the smallest target face I can aim at comfortably. Then I make sure that when I have good form the arrow goes where it is supposed to. With a hunting setup I like to go afield knowing that I have an accurate bow. Then, the only thing I have to worry about —other than being seen or smelled by the game—is how far away the animal is. If I know a bow will shoot exactly where I aim it, then

Bowhunter and three-time world archery champ Terry Ragsdale tunes his hunting setups and practices at longer ranges. "If I know a bow will shoot exactly where I aim it, then I don't have to worry about it so much when I am under the gun," he says.

I don't have to worry about it so much when I am under the gun."

Bob Fratzke, who has taken more than 24 trophy-class whitetails with a bow, also uses target practice to keep in top shooting form. "I love to shoot," he says, "so during the summer I shoot Wednesday-night league and a tournament every other weekend. During these tournaments, I'll shoot a lighter target bow with a lower draw weight and lighter arrows. I shoot instinctively, so my aiming points with this target setup are very similar to what they are with my hunting setup. For hunting, I shoot a heavier bow, more poundage and heavier arrows, but my points of aim are basically the same. It only takes me a few shots with my hunting setup to understand where I must aim."

Fratzke, the inventor of Winona Camouflage and a member of the Bear Archery Pro Staff, adds, "It basically comes down to this: Bowhunters must know their equipment, practice and be able to shoot well."

Surprisingly, none of these well-known bowhunters say they use 3-D tournaments to stay in top shooting form. This sport—which requires archers to shoot at three-dimensional animal targets at unknown distances—is growing both in shooter participation and industry enthusiasm. The Outdoor Trail Bowhunter Championship, for example, carries a cash and merchandise purse exceeding $150,000 and attracts more than 1,600 competitors.

The rise in popularity of 3-D shooting, however, has resulted in words of caution from some leading bowhunters. Chuck Adams, in a column published in *North American Hunter*, says: "Participation in 3-D tournaments has more than tripled during the past year alone. A close look at 3-D tournament results shows that most consistent, high-money winners use fast, short bows, extremely lightweight overdraw arrows and mechanical bowstring-release aids.

"Such combinations result in blistering arrow speed, which wins tournaments at unmarked yardage when non-broadhead arrows are used. However, I believe you do yourself a disservice if you confuse 3-D skills and gear with bowhunting needs. An inanimate foam-deer target cannot hear your ultra-fast, noisy bow, and flinch. A 3-D target cannot see or hear you fumble with a mechanical bowstring release.

"In 3-D tournaments, which require the use of arrows tipped by field points, you are not handicapped by the need to shoot large, speed-sensitive broadheads. And scoring a 'kill' on a foam-bodied buck does not require the deep arrow penetration best promoted by a sensible projectile weighing 6 to 8 grains per pound of draw weight. A bow and arrow setup shooting from 260 to 300 fps might win tournaments. However, high bow noise, erratic broadhead flight and less arrow energy can be a handicap in real hunting situations."

Selecting A Target

A wide variety of targets is available, and the one best for you depends on your setup and your personal preference. The most important factor with any target is that it must stop your arrow—first and foremost for safety reasons and also to keep from ripping the fletching from the shaft.

For typical practice with aluminum arrows and field points many targets will suffice. Standard hay bales piled three-high are used at many public shooting ranges and work well. For personal use, one of the many self-healing polyethylene foam targets works well for field points and broadheads.

Typically, polyethylene targets feature pre-cut bull's-eye centers which can be replaced after heavy use. The pre-cut center costs less than a new target. Two-inch-thick polyethylene foam with a 6-pound density should be sufficient for most compound bows shooting aluminum arrows. For crossbows and compounds exceeding 70-pound draw weights, select a 9-pound density target 2 inches thick. Bowhunters shooting thinner diameter carbon arrows should use a 4-pound-density, self-healing foam target at least 6 inches thick.

Most archery pro shops, mail order houses and discount chains sell these polyethylene targets. Heavy broadhead use, I have found, quickly depletes the target's effectiveness. I've shot out foam targets after one season. For heavy broadhead practice, I prefer a cubed block of Styrofoam. At present, a 2½-by-2½-by-2½-foot block is into its third season. These large blocks are available at many archery pro shops.

Target practice has also become more enjoyable and realistic with the introduction of simulated animal targets. These full-sized, three-dimensional targets are terrific for practice because a bowhunter can become familiar with the size of the animal and location of the vitals in order to determine the best shooting angles. On most 3-D targets the vitals are clearly marked and are replaceable. Some 3-D targets feature an ethafoam core which consistently stops broadhead-tipped arrows. Deer, elk and bear targets, for example, are available at large sporting goods stores and by mail order.

And what about Bob Atwill? He returned to Pennsylvania without a bull; however, he did have a better understanding of what it takes to be successful. He also returned home with an even deeper determination to return to Colorado and bag a certain bull elk.

14

Successful Scouting Strategies

Scouting is the activity that separates consistently successful bow-hunters from those who are only occasionally successful. Bows are important. Arrows are important. Broadheads are very important. Arrow flight is important. And practice is important if you plan to shoot well under pressure. But scouting—pinpointing the region where the animal lives and then finding a place from which you can hunt—is critical. If you fail to locate game, you may as well sit in a tree stand all season watching squirrels.

Some bowhunters invest off-season hours in monitoring their hunting area or researching a new area; some don't. A few bowhunters decipher game sign and understand what impact that sign will have during the season; others don't. Those who scout well and accurately decipher sign are most often the bowhunters who bag game. There's just no two ways about it.

To scout well does not require years of apprenticeship followed by a decade or two of serious effort—although it couldn't hurt. Scouting mostly involves common sense. Do your homework and get into the woods to look for sign. Scouting strategies used by successful bowhunters like Myles Keller, Chuck Adams, Bob Fratzke and Dwight Schuh will be covered.

Scouting Close To Home

Consider this scenario: You have been deer hunting for 15 years on public land close to home. You have bagged a few deer. However, last year the large number of bowhunters trying to hunt that public property reminded you more of firearm deer season. The public land was overcrowded. Nobody seemed to enjoy the hunt. And very few hunters bagged deer. At season's end, you decided to find some private property to hunt.

During the winter you talked with your hunting buddies about potential areas. You visited with people in sporting goods stores, and you kept an eye on the local newspaper's want ads. One Saturday morning the following spring, with a thermos full of coffee, and a county road map, you started driving the graveled back roads. After several hours you found a section of land that looked like the perfect white-tailed deer hideaway—far enough off the beaten path so that few bowhunters had access to it.

Then came a visit to the local courthouse to hunt down a plat book showing property boundaries and ownership. The section of land in question was found and the landowner's name located in the telephone directory. You called him during the week to set up a time to talk with him in person.

The next Saturday you drove out to the farm. Conversing with the landowner, you explained your appreciation for bowhunting and your interest in hunting on his property. Then, you showed him your NAHC Membership card which carries the hunter's code of ethics on the back.

The landowner granted you permission to hunt all wooded acres of his property. Even though he is not a hunter, he mapped out property lines and crop acreage. He also indicated where deer seem to concentrate, and where they feed on his crops. You drove home with a smile.

With the archery deer season still five months away, you should have ample time to thoroughly scout the property. But, where do you begin?

First, get a topographical (topo) map of the area (available at the local sporting goods store), as well as an aerial photo (available at the county extension office or the county courthouse). Study both the map and the photo at home. The topo map will show changes in elevation, including valleys and ravines. Thus, you can choose a small shelf or plateau or an old creek bed. Though the topo map indicates vegetation and swamps, it doesn't show vegetation type or density. This is where an aerial photo comes in handy. Use the aerial photo to find out whether that plateau is wooded or open with low brush. With a pencil, mark areas you want to investigate on your first scouting

When you're scouting during a hunt, you don't want to tip off the game that you're scouting. This bowhunter has positioned himself so he's not breaking the horizon and his movements are concealed.

Take advantage of spring scouting opportunities. With binoculars you can pinpoint game movement and feeding and bedding areas. Spring is also a good time to locate shed antlers.

mission, such as plateaus, draws or creek beds.

"By having both a topo map and an aerial photo map, a hunter can begin to get familiar with an area before he ever steps foot in it," says Myles Keller. "Then, when he scouts the area, rather than seeing just a maze of trees, he will begin to understand the area. He will have a mental picture of where he is and how everything is tied together." The fact that virtually every square mile in the country has been photographed from the air at one time or another makes it easier for this kind of scouting.

After developing that mental picture, investigate the area you marked on the topo map. Take along both maps, your mental picture of the area, binoculars and a pencil and compass on your first scouting mission. These tools should help you find your way around the property, investigate the area and record what you find.

"There isn't much danger in spooking deer in the spring," says Bob Fratzke. "Deer, at least in most populated areas, are what I call streetwise. A whitetail knows if a hunter has passed through an area 15 minutes earlier. During the spring, you need to get out there and understand the area and the deer. It's so much easier to see sign in the spring. For example, one year our whole state got dumped with snow over Halloween weekend. That snow covered all the pre-rut activity.

That sign was just waiting for hunters to discover when the snow melted.''

Spring and summer are good times to learn and understand game movement, feeding locations and bedding areas. Trails, of course, are the most obvious evidence of movement and should be especially easy to locate in the early spring when vegetation is still relatively short. Often these trails will connect the game's feeding and bedding areas. Investigate these trails. Deer beds are oblong ovals of matted grass or brush. Popular beds may be dirt-packed. (Most often these heavily used beds are on hillsides where game can see danger approaching from below.) Feeding areas will most often be found in open parks or agricultural fields.

When scouting, take the time to record on your map what you find. Experienced hunters mark on the map every rub, scrape, trail and bed. After a few scouting sessions, a pattern will probably begin to develop. That pattern may show a collection of beds in one area, and trails leading from those beds to the feeding area. From these early scouting trips you may already start choosing potential stand locations.

During spring scouting, you may find shed antlers. Sheds not only indicate the size and density in numbers of animals in the area, but they also show which bucks made it through the hunting season!

Antlered big game—elk, moose, deer, caribou—shed their racks every year; game with horns—sheep, mountain goat—do not. Although the time at which a buck or bull will drop his rack varies, it is generally after the rut. Big bucks will often drop their racks first because of a major decrease in hormone level following the rut. Smaller bucks which do not breed or breed very sparingly will usually lose their racks later. Whitetails typically lose their racks during the winter from late January into late February, and sometimes even in early March.

Spring scouting, therefore, is the perfect opportunity to spot shed antlers. Typically, sheds will be lying with points up on trails, in bedding areas or in feeding areas. Sometimes, both sides of a rack are found relatively close together—sometimes even in the same bed. Shed-antler hunting is not only a terrific reason to get out and scout, it sometimes evolves into a sport in itself. There's even growing interest in a record book for shed antlers.

"Summer is a time when bucks start to get a reasonable amount of horns," says Fratzke. "When that happens, I spend a lot of time on the road and in open fields glassing, looking for and watching deer movement.'' Glassing can be most productive around sunrise and

Even when you're on a guided big-game hunt, you can help your guide by glassing for game. Good quality spotting scopes or binoculars work well in this situation.

sunset—two times during the day when game animals are usually most active.

Summer is also a time to begin selecting potential stand locations. Consult your map showing beds, trails, feeding locations, scrapes and rubs. You most likely picked out a couple potential stand locations while scouting or shed-antler hunting.

Select three or four stand locations. If you will be hunting from a tree stand, climb each tree to check out shooting lanes. Provided you have approval from the landowner, trim and prune shooting lanes as early as possible. In areas where it's legal, some bowhunters install permanent stands well in advance of the hunting season to give game the opportunity to become accustomed to the stand. Also, where legal, ground blinds can be constructed well before the season opens.

By now, your scouting should be about complete. As the opener nears, avoid moving through the selected area if at all possible. Instead, glass from nearby roads or fields around sunrise and sunset.

It may sound strange, but another potentially good scouting time is during the hunting season when hunting pressure can push game into different behavior patterns.

"I think the most valuable scouting is near the end of the season," says Keller. "During that time it is very easy for me to see the scrapes and to determine deer densities (for next season).''

Keller often takes the opportunity provided by light rain or snow to still-hunt and scout areas that he would otherwise avoid. The rain and snow, Keller says, covers whatever human scent he may leave behind and quiets his approach and stalk.

Some hunters also scout after the hunting season to see where deer moved as the season progressed. In high-pressure areas, game can change bedding and feeding locations. An early-winter scouting session can reveal those changes. However, in colder climates, deer will yard up during the winter. Scouting winter deer yards can stress the deer. Man's intervention forces these animals to use up valuable energy and calories in seeking new, secure locations. If you want a healthy deer herd next fall, please avoid deer wintering areas.

Scouting Out Of Town

Consider this scenario: You and a hunting buddy have been bow-

Topnotch bowhunters like Myles Keller believe the most valuable scouting is near the end of the season. This hunter has found signs that deer are moving into this cornfield to feed.

hunting with some success for several years. You are both eager to try a big-game bowhunt in the West. The problem is the price tag; neither of you can afford the cost of such a hunt. Besides, you are both resourceful hunters and you both enjoy the satisfaction of doing something yourself. You opt for a do-it-yourself Western big-game bowhunt. The problem is selecting an area to hunt and scouting that area from home.

Dwight Schuh is recognized by many as a leading authority on back-country, do-it-yourself bowhunts. Although he lives in Idaho, Schuh is still 50 miles from the nearest mountain. No matter where he hunts, he must scout from home. "For me to get out and scout on a regular basis is very difficult," he explains. So Schuh has developed a system to research an area before the hunt. Here's how he does it.

"I try to find some type of pocket or drainage or mountain range that will not be heavily hunted by other people," he says. "My basic lead is word of mouth. When I go to sport shows or when I'm on the phone if I hear something that catches my ear I make a note of it. Sometimes it's an offhand comment like, 'I saw a lot of nice bulls up this drainage,' or 'I saw a lot of nice bucks up there.' I make a mental note of these things and write them down."

Following up on these clues, Schuh purchases public land maps of the area from the U.S. Forest Service and Bureau of Land Management. Maps from both of these agencies show access. Using these maps, Schuh will try to locate logging roads and access points into remote terrain. "Really what I am looking for are places where I will find undisturbed animals," he says. "I will study that map and try to find some places that I think might have the best opportunities for me to hunt. I try to find those types of places that I think other hunters might not consider because of poor road access due to private land blocking a certain area. If I can hike around that private land and get into the public land, I feel I might find some isolated country. Really what I am looking for are places where I will find some undisturbed animals."

Once Schuh finds a remote area which might harbor undisturbed animals, he purchases topo maps covering the area. Topo maps show terrain detail that may suggest pockets where game might hide undisturbed.

"I try to lay the groundwork before I get there," Schuh says. But he does not limit himself to a specific area or region to hunt. "I try to go into it with a totally open mind," he says. "I've marked the places on my maps with X's. These are the places that I want to look at. I'll try to go into one area and cover it as fast as I can, hiking and looking

Dwight Schuh, an authority on back-country bowhunts, says you should pinpoint potential spots on a topographical map before leaving home. The map with your comments becomes your road map during the hunt.

it over. If I'm elk hunting, I'll be bugling. If I'm deer hunting, I'll be rattling. And I will be using my binoculars, looking for animals, looking for sign and trying to evaluate the area. If I like what I'm seeing and there's a pretty good number of animals along with some action, I'm going to stay. I might end up spending my whole week hunting in one tiny little drainage.

"A cardinal rule is to stay mobile and be ready to move. Don't have any preconceptions about hunting a certain area." That's why Schuh likes to travel with a backpack; he can move with the game or into new regions to find the game population he desires.

A do-it-yourself, far-from-home hunt can be challenging and satisfying; however, expect to spend more days hunting than you might if you were hunting with a guide. "I find it rare for me to take a two- or three-day hunt," Schuh says. "I almost always take at least a week because a lot of times, the first two or three days are going to be just wheel-spinning, trying to figure something out."

Myles Keller uses topographic and aerial photo maps to pick out potential big-game hangouts before he does his scouting. This method has been fruitful for Keller.

Schuh says that an absolute minimum for a do-it-yourself deer hunt is one week. An absolute minimum for a do-it-yourself elk hunt is 10 days. ''It's going to take me four to five days in a new area to really narrow that down to what I want. In the normal sense of the word, I don't *scout*—because that, to me, means you're on the ground looking for sign. And I almost never do that. So I basically scout as I hunt. But I try to get a good, strong idea about what I'm getting into before I get there.''

Scouting During Guided Hunts

Even on guided hunts, some experienced hunters will scout for game and terrain that fits their hunting style. That's what veteran bowhunter Chuck Adams likes to do. ''I enjoy controlling as much as I can on a hunt, even on an outfitted hunt,'' he says. ''Some of my best friends are outfitters. I'm certainly not knocking outfitters, but I know how I hunt the best with a bow and arrow, so I like to do my own scouting to find the terrain that I am the most comfortable with. I know how I spot and stalk the best. The outfitter has no way of knowing what my preferred style is.''

Adams says he enjoys hunting broken areas that allow him to get within bow range before the animals see him. ''The average animal

This bowhunter (right) wanted to take part in the scouting, and expressed his desire to his guide before the hunt started. It's also important to have a guide that has bowhunting experience.

that I see never has the slightest chance to see more than my head and my shoulders," he says. "Some other bowhunters prefer to take a stand or slip along the same sidehill as the animal and use foliage instead of solid terrain like rocks and ridge line. So for me, I think it's very important to do my own scouting once I get there. And then to communicate to my outfitter the areas that I prefer to hunt."

The key for scouting on guided hunts is to make certain that the guide or outfitter knows up front, before the hunt, that this is what you prefer. "If I've done my research," Chuck says, "I already know that my outfitter is going to be amiable to my suggestions."

Successful big-game scouting does not require a doctorate in animal behavior or a decade of experience. Like so much in bowhunting, it simply requires common sense and determination. If you combine those two qualities with the techniques and strategies just described, you'll be on your way to bowhunting success.

15

Bowhunters: Masters Of Camouflage

Reporting on his field-test of a new camouflage outfit, an NAHC Member said: "While field-testing Liberty Hide'n Pine camouflage, I had a man walk past me at about 7 feet away. He stopped and looked at my tracks leading off the road, and looked up. When he saw me, he jumped about a foot off the ground. 'Nice camo,' he managed to say." That's what camouflage should do.

Bowhunters must be masters of camouflage. They must be able to blend in so well with their surroundings that they appear to disappear, even to another person who is following their footprints.

Bowhunters must wear clothes that are quiet. Clothes that "crinkle" when you draw could produce the game-spooking sound that leaves you watching the backside of a fleeing big-game animal.

Years ago, bowhunters had two options when it came to choosing a camouflage pattern: military camo or military camo. Earth-tone wool garments also were used by many bowhunters.

Today, there are dozens of camouflage patterns. No matter where you hunt—no matter what forest or prairie or marsh—chances are there is a camouflage pattern that will work well for you. Some patterns are even available with different colors and tones for different seasons.

Selecting A Camouflage Pattern

If I had been the hunter who walked up to the NAHC Member, I would have asked him what pattern he was wearing. Then I would have turned around and high-tailed it immediately to the local sporting goods store.

Determining which pattern works best for you depends upon where and when you hunt. Here are two simple, unscientific techniques you can use for selecting the best camouflage pattern.

The surefire way is to call your hunting partners, and tell them to grab all of the different patterns from their closets and meet you near your favorite hunting spot. Grab your own patterns, then go out to the area where you hunt. Be sure to do this when the colors and vegetation cover are similar to what they are like during the hunting season.

Place the different camouflage patterns on limbs or brush, then walk away some 20 to 30 yards. Turn and look at the patterns. What you see might surprise you. Some patterns will blend together and appear as a solid-colored coat, shirt or pants while others will effectively break up the outline of the garment.

The trick is to place the garment in a setting that tends to duplicate your hunting situation. If you hunt exclusively from a tree stand, then hang your clothes next to the trunk of the tree or even up on a limb. Then walk away, seeing what the pattern looks like from different distances. What you will discover could surprise you.

On a Western pronghorn hunt, I thought I had a good camouflage pattern. Up close, it was easy to see the pattern, and against the prairie grass it blended in just fine.

Looking at the photos after the hunt, however, I soon discovered that the pattern, from a distance, disappeared. My camouflage coat that looked so good up close, turned into a dark, almost-solid color when viewed from a distance. While this pattern would work for tree-stand hunting, it wasn't appropriate for the open prairie.

The second way is even easier, and you can do it by yourself. Just drive to the parking lot of a public hunting area that is popular with bowhunters who are required to be out of the woods soon after sunset. Watch as those hunters walk out of the woods. There is still sufficient light to see and you can get an idea of the patterns that are most effective in that hunting environment.

These two methods are not scientific, and they are not exciting. But, they can be extremely effective ways of determining which pattern works best under specific hunting conditions. You need to be sure that the pattern works before you get into a hunting situation.

Selecting Silent Camouflage

Big-game animals have us beat hands down when it comes to

Literally dozens of effective camouflage patterns are now available for bowhunters to use in almost any location. While effectively disguising and breaking the hunter's outline, camouflage material must also be silent.

Can you find him? This bowhunter who is wearing Mossy Oak's Treestand pattern blends into the background. The camouflage breaks up the hunter's outline so he can remain unnoticed.

keen senses. They not only can see much better than human beings can, but they can hear much better, too.

To be an effective camouflage system, it must allow the bowhunter to move silently when he stands up and, especially, when he draws. If a camouflage garment doesn't allow a bowhunter to do this, it limits his opportunities for success.

The good news, of course, is that there are many silent comfortable fabrics available today. Cotton for warm weather and wool for cold weather provide freedom of movement with little or no noise.

Bowhunters wear a variety of hunting hats. Whichever one you are most comfortable wearing is the one to use. But remember, the ever-popular baseball-cap style might not lend itself well to bowhunting. Most bowhunters I have met draw the bowstring to within 1½ to 2½ inches of their forehead. The brim of a baseball cap could get in the way of your bowstring—that's not the type of distraction you need when you are ready to draw on any game animal. Whatever hat you prefer, practice with it. Draw back and anchor from a standing, sitting, kneeling and bent over position to make sure the hat will not interfere with the bowstring when you're at full draw. Also, make sure that it will stay on your head regardless of your position.

And one of the most easily overlooked areas of camouflage, believe it or not, is a bowhunter's ankles. Stand and look at yourself in a mirror and you don't even see your ankles. But sit down. See how your pant legs creep up? Now imagine a game animal almost directly below you and how easy it would be for it to catch a glimpse of your socks, or even worse your *white* cotton socks. Better yet wear white cotton socks while you're in your tree stand. Put on your safety belt, then sit down and have a hunting buddy look up from below. Sure, he won't always be in the right position to spot the whites of your cotton socks, but he will from certain positions. There is no easy answer to camouflaging your ankles, because I have never seen a good pair of camouflaged socks, but earth-tone wool socks will work. Another possible solution is to tighten your pants legs around your ankles, either with a draw string found inside the cuffs of some pants or with short lengths of tape.

Camouflage As A Total System

For bowhunters to be successful, they typically must be within 20 yards of the game they are hunting. To get that close and not be de-

Camouflage paint will effectively break up the solid color and shine of a bowhunter's face. If you don't use face paint—which can be washed off with soap—your other option is a camouflaged headnet.

Two bowhunters have set up behind decoys in order to try to get a short-range shot at a pronghorn. Note how the camouflage worn by the hunter on the left becomes a solid color at a distance. The hunter should have checked that before going into the field.

tected, bowhunters must have more than just a good camouflage outfit. They must have a total camouflage system.

The hands and head are the parts of your body which move the most when you are in the tree stand. Consider camouflaging them in some way. Your hands are the objects that will move the most when you draw your bow. At the very least, you should wear a camouflaged glove on your bow hand. Covering the hand that draws the bow is a decision the shooter has to make.

Finger shooters, for example, may find it impossible to shoot well, even with very thin gloves. However, some gloves feature a cut across the palm, so the fingers can slip out of the glove in order to make the shot.

Release-aid shooters may be able to wear gloves comfortably without incident. If you decide to shoot with camouflage gloves, practice shooting with that glove. A glove can change the feel of your release whether you shoot fingers or with a release.

Headnets are another possibility as part of a complete camouflage system. Some bowhunters can shoot well while wearing a headnet; others cannot. Practice shooting while wearing a headnet to see if it impacts your shooting performance.

If you can't wear a headnet, an option is to apply camouflage face paint. Even streaks of camouflage paint break up the solid skin color. The whole face does not need to be painted, and the paint can be easily washed off with soap and water.

Camouflage Your Hunting Rig

Bowhunters must be certain to camouflage those objects which move the most when they are hunting. Their bow-and-arrow setup, of course, moves the most—especially when game is close. Successful camouflage should extend to your bow and arrows. Most hunting bows are painted with a camouflage pattern at the factory. If not, bowhunters should try spray painting their bow, or covering it with some type of camouflage tape or sleeve.

Bow accessories should also be camouflaged wherever possible. Accessories like sights, quivers and overdraws are often painted non-glare black. That flat black color can be sufficient for camouflaging these accessories. However, inspect them periodically. Sometimes

By glassing and then stalking this free-ranging bison, PSE President Pete Shepley was able to get close enough to bring the beast down with an arrow. Using light-colored fletch helps the hunter identify arrow placement.

that non-glare black finish will wear off, leaving a shiny metal surface. If that happens, camouflage the accessory with paint or tape.

The color of your arrow fletch is another accessory to consider when camouflaging your hunting rig. Some bowhunters prefer to have a red or orange fletch to see their arrow hits better. Sometimes, bowhunters can see a brightly colored fletch as the arrow enters the animal. Other bowhunters, however, prefer fletch that is earth-tone in color to blend into the surroundings; they think it is less likely to be seen by the animal when the bow is drawn. Camouflaged arrows can be extremely difficult to find if the arrow misses the animal or goes completely through. Fletch color is basically a matter of personal preference.

A Professional's Thoughts On Camouflage

Ev Tarrell is the hunting clothing buyer/designer for Cabela's, a major sporting goods outlet and mail order firm headquartered in Nebraska. In one year, he typically reviews and evaluates more than 40 different camouflage patterns. He will then select more than two dozen patterns, and match those patterns to a specific garment made from a specific fabric. Plus Tarrell is a serious bowhunter. "The secret to selecting an effective camouflage pattern is to analyze the environment that you will be hunting in most often," he says. "Look at the colors on the ground, in the trees and against the tree trunks. Then review the different camouflage patterns available."

Tarrell says there are more than 40 different camouflage patterns to choose from, and adds, "There is definitely a perfect area in the country for each type of camouflage available." He added that on a macro scale, certain camouflage patterns work best in certain regions of the country—Mossy Oak and Hide 'n Pine in the Southeast, Realtree in the Midwest, Realtree All-Purpose and Mossy Oak Treestand in the Northeast and, depending on the area, desert camouflage out West.

"Quietness is another important factor bowhunters must consider when selecting camouflage clothing," adds Tarrell. "Most bowhunters hunt from tree stands, and in those situations a big-game animal must be in close for the bowhunter to have a chance at success. When an animal is within bow range, quietness is the key. Tree stands get you out of a big-game animal's sight plane. The secret is to be able to come to full draw when the animal doesn't see you without making a sound the animal will hear."

The amount of noise clothing makes, Tarrell explains, is determined by its construction and by the material of which it is made.

The bowhunter in the center of this photo concealed his movements in coming to full draw by remaining still until the deer's vision was blocked by tree trunks. The deer remain unaware of his presence.

When deciding what clothes to wear for bowhunting, study the construction and the material. A bowhunter can move quietly while wearing chamois, fleece, brushed cotton and wool. On the other hand, waterproof fabrics or fabrics with stiff liners may not allow a bowhunter to lift an arm, much less draw a bow, without making too much noise.

The best place to test whether your hunting garments make any noise when you stand, turn or draw your bow is before you ever buy them. When trying on hunting clothes in a sporting goods store or an archery pro shop, go to the quietest part of the store and slowly draw back. Do you hear anything? Listen again for the rubbing of fabric or scraping of a button or zipper. Then squat down and slowly stand up. How much noise do the garments make? Determine, as best you can at the store, whether an animal could hear the noise when you draw. Remember, chances are good that the animal will be close.

Some clothes, unfortunately, are noisier than others. You must decide if the added comfort from the clothes is worth the risk. Waterproof clothing, for example, is typically noisy, and there doesn't seem to be a lot you can do about it. You can put another quieter garment over the outside of a waterproof garment to muffle the sound of your movements. That will help, but consider what influence those clothing layers might have on your shooting ability.

"You give up a little bit by having a waterproof insert in your hunting garment," says Tarrell. "You must weigh the advantages of the waterproof, breathable garment against the disadvantages of a slightly noisier draw. You want a garment that allows you to hunt when you want to hunt, not when the weather says you can hunt."

"The bottom line," Tarrell says, "is to select and to wear the quietest possible garments that will do the job. There are so many different climates and conditions under which bowhunters go afield that it is impossible to recommend 'the best' garment, fabric or pattern. Instead, select chamois or brushed cottons for warm-weather hunting, poly-cotton blends for the early season when it is cooler and wools and fleeces for the late season when it is colder. Wool and fleece offer tremendous advantages in insulation."

Asked what he thinks is the most common mistake bowhunters make when camouflaging themselves for the hunt, Tarrell says they sometimes forget about the little parts. "A bowhunter might spend his money on a camouflage coat and pants but fail to think about camouflaging his bow, arrow, hands and face," Tarrell explains. "Bowhunters are very good at covering 90 percent of themselves with effective camouflage. Yet the 10 percent that some bowhunters miss are the most important areas. When you spot a camouflaged hunter in the woods, what is the first thing you see? Often it's his face. Even a little bit of paint will help to break up the solid color of a person's face. And the hands move the most during the most critical time —one hand draws back the bowstring and the other is pointing at the animal." Tarrell also sees to it that he takes the shine out of all bow-mounted accessories, like his sight pins. He uses a light coat of flat matte spray paint to dull such accessories.

"How you camouflage the remaining 10 percent is a matter of personal preference," concludes Tarrell. "Bowhunters need to decide what is most comfortable and effective for their situation."

Ten Quick Camo Tips From Haas Outdoors

1. Match pattern to background, and consider wearing different patterns on top and bottom. For instance: You could combine Treestand top and Bottomland pants for an effective camouflage.

Often two different camouflage patterns will work in one hunting area. Note how the pattern to the left blends in with the dark trees while the lighter pattern works well in dried grass.

2. Always use camo paint or covering on hands and face. These two parts of the body move more than any other while hunting.

3. Cover anything shiny: watch, buttons, snaps and zippers. These small details sometimes demand great attention.

4. Purchase pants 2 to 3 inches longer than needed. This will keep light-colored socks and boots from standing out.

5. Wear boots with dark soles. They are sometimes the first thing an animal will see if a hunter is sitting at ground level.

6. Avoid direct sunlight. If possible face west in the morning and east in the afternoon.

7. Think about your intentions when you pick a spot to sit down. From 40 yards in, you want to blend. From 40 yards out, you concentrate more on breaking your outline.

8. Set up on edges. Avoid getting in the middle of thick cover. This hampers your vision in seeing game; they like to travel edges anyway.

9. Keep your outline as low as possible. Avoid the animal's eye level. Scrunch down while on the ground, and get 15 feet or higher when using a tree stand.

10. Use face paint to touch up around your eyes, even if you are wearing a face net. It keeps down the shine.

16

Bowhunting Whitetails

Probably no big-game animal in North America riles the hunting spirit in more hunters than white-tailed deer. The whitetail is by far the most popular big-game animal in North America—perhaps in the world. Nearly 80 percent of NAHC Members, for example, hunt whitetails. That's nearly twice the number who hunt black bear—the second most popular game animal.

Each fall hundreds of thousands of bowhunters pursue this popular white-tailed animal. These hunters, as you know from previous chapters, have their choice of the most sophisticated, scientifically advanced hunting gear imaginable. Bow risers are machined from bars of solid aluminum. Arrow shafts are straight within $^{15}/_{1000}$ of an inch. Camouflage patterns are scientifically designed to represent 17 percent gray—the same percent on average, as in nature. Eccentrics are refined and redesigned by computers to produce maximum energy. In short, bowhunting gear has improved significantly during the past decade.

Bowhunter success on whitetails, as indicated in Chapter 1, averages about 15 percent. According to harvest statistics released by 26 states and compiled by the 28th Annual Northeast Deer Technical Committee (NDTC), the annual success rate for bowhunters taking whitetails is less than 15 percent (actually 14.85 percent). Average bowhunter success for deer is 7 percent in Pennsylvania; 5 in New York; 10 in Texas; 12 in Missouri. According to the report, the highest success rate was 36.5 percent in Georgia; the lowest was 3 percent in Maine and New Hampshire. Bowhunters can buy archery equipment that is shadow quiet and laser accurate. They can camouflage with the most effective patterns that money can buy. Yet, according to NDTC, a bowhunter will harvest only one deer every 6.6 years, on average; after 13 years, he will have two deer.

Granted, that's not bad. Granted, success isn't everything. Granted, bowhunters enjoy the additional challenge and accept a lower success rate. However, most bowhunters want to bag more animals, especially more and bigger whitetails. Perhaps then, in addition to shooting the most advanced hunting gear, bowhunters need to bolster their understanding of the game animals they hunt.

Even though bowhunters' nationwide average is a 15 percent success rate hunting whitetails, one bowhunter has taken 27 during the past 30 years. Better yet, these 27 whitetails are trophy-class animals. Meanwhile, another well-known bowhunter has harvested two dozen trophy-class whitetails near his hometown. What's their secret? "Basically, successful bowhunting requires a lot of hard work." says the second successful bowhunter. "It means getting ready long before the season starts."

This is an attempt to give you an in-depth look at the tactics, techniques and thoughts of these two successful whitetail bowhunters. You'll get a look at their scouting techniques—what they look for when they scout an area and when they select a spot to hunt. You will also learn some of their most productive hunting strategies. In addition, later in this chapter, aggressive deer hunting techniques like rattling and calling will be examined.

How credible are these experts? You decide.

The first is Myles Keller. With 18 Pope-and-Young record whitetailed deer and nine other trophy-class whitetails taken with a bow, Keller has shot more record-book whitetails than any bowhunter in history, ever. His accomplishment dwarfs the fact that a single P&Y whitetail is usually considered the achievement of a lifetime.

Our second expert is Bob Fratzke. Fratzke has harvested the 24 trophy-class whitetails, and has been bowhunting for the past 36 years.

Myles Keller's Whitetail Strategies

Keller has this advice for whitetail bowhunters: Avoid areas with high hunting pressure, and give whitetails the credit they deserve.

"Years ago I could drive around and scout for deer," says Keller, who lives in southeastern Minnesota. "I could find a good area and

White-tailed deer are without a doubt the most-sought-after big-game animal in North America. Despite the advances in bowhunting equipment, only one in seven bowhunters will take a whitetail during a season.

set up on a deer fairly easily. And just by covering the basics, like staying clean and watching my approach to the stand, I could meet with success. However, there are many more bowhunters in the woods today. I think the bigger bucks are more in tune and more educated to the fact that they are being hunted because of this higher hunting pressure.''

The solution, Keller says, is to avoid heavily hunted areas. ''I have to leave the area where I live to hunt,'' he explains. ''With extreme amounts of hunting pressure, you can't rely on your hunting skills to get you a deer. I know this sounds like old hat for most bowhunters, but it's one of those truths we must realize. You can have the best setup and you can be careful about everything, but if you have hunters driving the woods and disturbing the deer, you are not going to get the opportunities you need to be successful. You must hunt an area where you can apply your knowledge.''

Most hunters do not want to hear this, because they have their favorite, close-to-home hunting spots, such as a wood lot or a friend's place they've hunted for years. Of course, there's nothing wrong with continuing to hunt those areas, provided the hunter realizes that he may not be successful as often as he would like.

For those bowhunters who would rather follow Keller's advice and look for an unpressured hunting location, the first step is to locate regions that harbor the quality of bucks you desire. Consult record books published by Boone and Crockett and Pope and Young to learn where trophy deer are being taken. These books can help you pinpoint regions and counties. You must be in an area that has produced high-quality deer in order to get a chance at taking one, Keller says. Hunting on land that does not harbor such animals is one of the classic mistakes made by otherwise capable hunters.

''If you go someplace like South Dakota or Iowa during the early season, there is a good chance you will have an entire area to yourself,'' Keller says. ''In these states, it's like turning the clock back 20 years. You just don't have the hunter population that you do in other states.''

Keller also believes bowhunters must give white-tailed deer the credit they deserve. ''The most common mistake,'' he said, ''is that bowhunters do not realize they are hunting a superior animal that is very smart. Give that animal credit. To be successful, bowhunters must get rid of the attitude that they are just going out hunting in an area where there is a lot of good sign. We need to let the advice of other successful hunters really sink in. For instance, bowhunters often hear that deer have a good nose; however, hunters tend to put that

In order to get a shot at large bucks, bow-hunters are advised to avoid areas with intense hunting pressure. Todd Amenrud took this trophy-class whitetail in Canada's Alberta province.

fact in the back of their minds. It's there, but often they just don't let it really sink in that the animal is sharp and has a terrific sense of smell. Once you let that sink in, you realize that you must put in some effort to limit and contain your scent. Bowhunting has a lot to do with attitude.''

When it comes to keeping his scent to a minimum, Keller uses Scent Shield. "I take a bath in it," he says. "I have my clothes washed in that and I keep them separate, especially that outer layer, from my other garments. Depending upon the temperature, I may not put on the outer layer until I get into my stand, but most often I'll put it on when I get out of my truck. Once at my stand, I'll use a towel of Scent Shield on higher perspiration areas.

"An illustration of how it works would be if you had a lid on a gas can," Keller explains. "As soon as you crack the lid you can smell the gas. The molecules are in the air. Anything we smell has to be in a molecular state suspended in the air. Scent Shield locks onto the human odor molecule and won't let it turn to a gas.''

Scent is just one of the important considerations. Another is attitude. It is a mistake to hunt whitetails half-heartedly, expecting to meet with success. "People who set their stand up in a promising area to 'see what happens' tend to over-hunt that stand," Keller says. "We've all heard somebody say they are going to sit on a stand to see if the area is any good. Bowhunters cannot afford to do this.

"I go to my stand just as confident as I can be," he continues. "I will believe there is an extremely good chance I will kill a deer off that stand that very day. I'm not going to compromise an entire day or evening of hunting by going at it half-heartedly. We must face the fact that we're going to have very few opportunities off any given stand. So when I take that stand, I'm going to do it when everything is just right. I must restrict myself because over-hunting a good stand for a big buck will most often leave you empty-handed."

Keller's confidence comes, in part, from his ability to pinpoint and understand white-tailed deer habitat. "When I'm scouting an area, in the back of my mind I'm looking for a density of deer where a buck could hole up," he says. "I put a fair amount of merit on good-sized rubs. I'm looking for evidence such as a good rub in the area. And here's the trick when you scout after the season; you have to determine that the sign you are looking at is relatively close to the security area for a given buck. People talk about a home range for a buck of one square mile. Well, I think a buck's home range may be three square miles, or more. Some of them are—and this is just my opinion—pretty much 'homebodies' in tune to a family-type situation.

"Other bucks are a little more nomadic," he continues. "I think whether a buck is nomadic or a homebody has a lot to do with the herd structure, dominance, buck populations and doe populations that he was exposed to early in life. Some of them, I believe, feel comfortable and confident in their current herd. Those deer are what I call homebodies."

During a light rain, Keller usually goes out on a combination still-hunt and scouting mission, especially if he has an area he wants to see but hasn't, because he didn't want to disturb it. "A light rain or snow erases any scent that you might leave behind," he says. "Plus, when snow or light rain is falling, deer don't seem to be able to lock onto you as quickly. You get away with more. Not only because it's quiet. Their vision is just not as sharp. It's like there is a curtain in front of them. They don't get that clear view. I have gotten away with a lot under these conditions, and I know that it is not just because it is quieter. If I'm stalking and a deer looks my way, I will freeze. Often, I'll get away with it during these conditions."

Although it's a popular notion, Keller says he does not hunt one particular buck. "That's a common misconception," he says. "It sounds good, and I wish a person could really be that good. I do get drawn into that once in a while, but it's best to have an alternative buck. The minute you try to hunt one buck, you really get wrapped up in it.

Myles Keller finds a "fair amount" of merit in good-sized rubs. This hunter has found a rub that fits that category on an 8-inch-diameter tree trunk. Keller warns hunters, however, not to overhunt a spot.

"If you love to hunt, you are going to have an alternate place so you don't over-hunt the main buck," he says. "A lot of times when I am hunting the alternate buck, I will think about what might be going on at the other stand. This can be frustrating, but this gives me and the stand a break. Plus, I still have the opportunity to hunt and maybe compare a second buck to the main one. Then, all of a sudden, it's like a light bulb. You suddenly see that you are doing two or three things wrong with the setup on the main buck. If you over-hunt one particular buck, pretty soon you just won't see him at all."

Fratzke's Successful Strategies

"Basically, successful bowhunting requires a lot of hard work," Fratzke says. "It means getting ready long before the season starts. It requires knowing an area not only during the hunting season, but also during the spring and summer."

Fratzke says his most productive hunting strategy is to put out "licking sticks" early in the spring. By fall, many of these will become scrapes over which Fratzke can hunt. "You are more or less making the deer stop where you want them to," he explains. "You are creating the opportunity, and you're doing it in the spring.

"A licking branch to a deer is just like a fire hydrant to a dog," Fratzke explains. "When a deer walking down the trail encounters a branch about 6 feet off the ground, it will often stop and lick the branch and urinate below it. In some prime hunting territory, I've found there is an absence of overhanging branches that are 6 feet off the ground near well-used trails. What I do then, is to bend over a nearby sapling and tie it off with bailing wire wrapped loose enough so the wire won't choke off the branch.

"In the spring, I will kick the leaves away on the ground below this branch to simulate a scrape," he continues. "If there are no saplings along the trail and if I am hunting private land, I will cut a small sapling and staple it to another tree with fence post staples. As that licking branch is used during the spring and summer, I will periodically add another branch or sapling over the top of the old one. What I'm doing is making the deer stop where I want them to. That is a spot where I can set up a tree stand."

Although a tree stand gets Fratzke above the deer's immediate line of sight, he is not high enough to be safe from their keen sense of smell. "I personally don't think there is anything you can put on that will completely cover the human scent," he says. "I keep myself as clean as possible. That includes taking a shower every time before I go out, even in the evening when I go out after work. When I'm out hunting I have a hard time not perspiring, so I try to dress as lightly as possible. One product I believe really works are these disposable towels from Scent Shield. I just wipe myself clean with one, especially my face and any exposed skin, once I am on my tree stand."

Aggressive Hunting Techniques

Some bowhunters hunt whitetails aggressively, preferring to bring bucks in by rattling or grunting. "I first started rattling whitetails nine years ago when I lived in Colorado," says Wayne Carlton of Carlton Calls & Huntin' Stuff. "Friends of mine back in South Carolina were having such good luck with rattling that I decided to give it a try.

"We've been real successful at calling in whitetails, and the further I go with it, the more successful we become," he continues. "It's to the point now that when we go out to call deer, if I don't call one in, I think something is wrong."

When rattling whitetails, you're using the antlers to create excitement and get the deer's attention from as far away as possible. "That means I'm rattling loud and often," he says. "I'll do this for 1 to 1½ minutes. Then I'll wait for 20 minutes."

If you catch a buck just right, he should come in fairly fast. "In the cases where I have been able to watch them, big bucks come smoking in," he says. "Small bucks will come in and play peek-a-

By watching closely, this hunter has discovered a scrape on the edge of his woodlot. Veteran bowhunter Bob Fratzke "creates" scrapes by putting a licking branch about 6 feet above a deer trail.

boo. But every year that I have tried rattling deer in I've been able to connect. In South Carolina, we set up in seven locations and rattled in deer five times.

"Rattling for whitetails will work especially well as soon as the velvet starts coming off their antlers. That's when they start to establish herd dominance. The other good time is during the rut. At other times, you might go out for 10 days and nothing happens."

Another aggressive deer-hunting technique is to use a deer call. Carlton prefers an aggressive, piercing deer grunt. "I think the deer you get to come to the casual type grunts are the deer that are ready to come in right at that moment," he says. "The problem is, there are very few deer in the woods at any one time that are primed and ready to come in to a casual grunt. Instead, I prefer a real aggressive-type call, where you work the deer up to a point that he comes in, even though he isn't quite ready."

An aggressive grunt is a much faster and louder sound. "It should be a sharp, piercing call," says Carlton, "one that almost makes your ears hurt. And I don't think you should wait 10 or 15 minutes between grunting. If you can watch a deer coming in to a grunt, a lot of times they will run toward the sound, then stop. It's like they are waiting for you to grunt again before they come any closer. That's why I grunt so much. There are too many other sounds in the woods that can occupy a deer's mind if you don't do something to continue to bring him in."

NAHC Members interested in hunting whitetails aggressively should purchase one of the many good instructional cassette tapes available at local archery pro shops. These contain examples of proper rattling and grunting sounds and techniques.

"Hunting whitetails aggressively, whether calling or rattling, gives you the opportunity to bring a buck to you—a location he might otherwise not visit," says Carlton. "Plus, that buck will come in alert and ready. For pure bowhunting excitement, that's hard to beat."

Eddie Salter of Eddie Salter Calls says, "We are just finding out that deer are very vocal animals, and they communicate with each other by using sounds such as bleats, blats and grunts." They make these sounds year-round, not just during the rut. Primarily, the best time to use a deer grunt call is in the rut or mating season. But, it can be used year-round with great results.

"I travel all over the United States giving seminars on deer calling techniques," Salter continues. "And probably the most asked question is 'How far can a deer hear?' On a cool, crisp morning with no wind blowing and moderate cover, a deer can probably hear up to 200 yards, maybe farther. Two factors determine this: cover, which I am referring to as trees and undergrowth, and wind direction. If a stiff wind is blowing and you're downwind of said deer, then he or she would have to be mighty close to hear a grunt call. On the other hand, if you were upwind, then there's no telling how far they could hear the call."

While Carlton advocates loud, aggressive calling, Salter prefers a quieter grunt. "If deer were vocalizing these grunts very loud, then we would have put two and two together a lot sooner than now."

Another common question is: How many times do I grunt? "That is personal preference," Salter says. "I prefer to grunt three times, wait 10 to 15 seconds and repeat it. Then I wait 5 to 10 minutes before repeating this method again. I've had tremendous results doing this. Matter of fact, a 12-pointer and an 8-pointer fell for this method last year."

Although many hunters prefer using tree stands, Salter likes to hunt on the ground. "This allows me to move around from place to

The best times for rattling in whitetails are when the velvet is coming off the bucks' racks and, of course, during the rut when the bucks are extremely aggressive.

Eddie Salter, a professional deer-call maker, finds that deer can hear a grunt tube, like the one being used here, as far as 200 yards away. Salter prefers to hunt on the ground when he's using the grunt tube so he can be more mobile.

Experts say deer may be able to hear grunt calls up to 200 yards away. Note that this buck, although his head is turned away, has rotated his ears to pick up sounds coming from behind him.

place and possibly get closer to the deer so they can hear the call," he says. "Grunting is a means of communication for white-tailed deer.

"As an example, a dominant buck has marked off his domain and has more or less got a boundary which he has set up and he claims every doe in that area," Salter explains. "When we come into this area grunting, we are letting this dominant buck know that we're looking for a doe and if it takes fighting for one, then so be it. That's why a lot of times people recall bucks coming in with their hair standing up. I've had the opportunity to harvest several bucks by using the grunt call, and believe me it works."

Hunting From Ground Blinds

Ground blinds can be used in conjunction with tree stands. In Alabama, while bowhunting whitetails with representatives of an archery manufacturer, I hunted from a tree stand over two food plots. In front of me was a clover field. To my right was standing corn. From the stand I saw deer every night. However, they fed in the clover field at least 50 yards away, never offering me a shooting opportunity.

Watching the deer from my tree stand, I noticed that most deer entered the field near one corner of the standing corn. During midday, I set up a small ground blind four rows deep in the standing corn. I bent the stalks back to open up shooting lanes. Late that afternoon, numerous deer passed within 25 yards of that ground blind.

On the barren plains of some Western states, ground blinds provide cover where there is none. On a bowhunt in South Dakota, for example, I found sage brush that was between 12 and 18 inches high. We used a lightweight portable ground blind to provide cover and camouflage for hunting pronghorns. We were filming an episode for the NAHC's television show, "North American Outdoors," and at one point used the blind to conceal the camera, cameraman, tripod and sound man. Such blinds cost less than $100, and are lightweight, portable and effective.

17

Successful Tree-Stand Hunting

Inventions revolutionizing the sport of bowhunting, such as porta-ble tree stands, are few and far between. Not long ago, most people hunted from ground blinds or permanent stands. Today, you would be hard-pressed to find more than a handful of bowhunters who have not used a tree stand. Even in the West, where still-hunting and stalking are popular, bowhunting guides are starting to put hunters on tree stands over watering holes and along well-used trails.

Tree stands get the hunter and his movements out of the game an-imal's immediate line of sight. And with the hunter high above the ground, his scent has an opportunity to dissipate into the air—not on the ground. Another advantage is that lightweight portable tree stands allow bowhunters to penetrate areas and set up in minutes. Today, tree stands play an important role in successful hunting strategies through-out North America.

Successful tree-stand hunters, just like all successful bowhunters, cover every facet of the technique. With patience and attention to de-tail, they select tree-stand placement, tree-stand height, shooting lanes and tree-stand approach.

Three Types Of Tree Stands

The three basic types of tree stands are climbing, fixed location and permanent. A climbing tree stand is just that—a tree stand with which a hunter can climb a tree. Climbing tree stands typically have a metal bracket that encircles the tree. The hunter straps his feet into the stand and climbs the tree by hooking the metal bracket around the tree. The place on the stand where the hunter straps in his feet becomes the tree stand's platform.

Today, many climbing tree stands have a rubber or protective coating on all the metal hooks that come in contact with the tree. This protects trees, especially in heavily used locations. Some states have passed laws restricting the use of tree stands without this protective coating. (Consult your state's regulations for more information.)

A fixed-location stand must be raised into the tree and securely fastened. These stands can be extremely lightweight and portable.

Permanent tree stands are most popular on private land. Hunter education courses typically discourage the use of permanent tree stands because the stands are most often constructed of wood and nails. Over time, that wood can rot and the nails can work their way out of the tree. Plus, permanent stands are often constructed by nailing boards to two or three trees. When the wind blows, those trees sway independently, stretching and pulling at the boards and nails. This often results in a creaky stand. Unless permanent stands are solidly constructed, they can be the sources of game-spooking noise when you shift your weight.

Successful Tree-Stand Hunting Techniques

Once Myles Keller finds a spot harboring big, trophy-class deer, he places a tree stand in a likely area. In general, Keller prefers to be at least 12 feet off the ground. Most of the time, he is 18 to 20 feet. Stand height is determined by two factors: background cover and shooting lanes. "I don't want to do any more pruning or cutting than I have to," he says. "So as I climb the tree with my tree stand, not only am I concerned about getting above the deer's general line of vision, but I am looking for shooting lanes and opportunities. Sometimes I determine tree-stand location based on the number of shooting lanes I will have without any extensive pruning."

Keller says most of his shots from a tree stand average between 12 and 14 yards. "I don't have a favorite tree stand make or model," he says. "Some of the small, light tree stands I'll stick on my back and take off for the day scouting. Then, if it's 3 o'clock and almost time to go back to the truck, I'll throw it up somewhere and try to hunt.

"When I place the stand," Keller explains, "I stop and think first of all about wind. In some situations, you have predominant wind. You have valleys and hills and you are going to have changing winds. I think of all the things that I'm going to encounter when I set up a

A climbing tree stand makes the stand's placement a lot easier. Not only does this stand climb trees but it also will move around limbs that would stop most other climbing stands.

Today's tree stands provide a modest amount of comfort while giving the hunter an elevated view. With a tree stand, a bowhunter can be well above the deer's normal line of sight, and in good position for a killing shot.

stand. In other words, I don't set up a stand like other hunters who gravitate to a scrape or a phenomenal amount of sign. My first priority is I want to keep the odds as high as I can. I want to get a shot at that deer, but I want to be a little bit versatile with my approach. A lot of times I'll set up my stand so that not only will I be able to approach it when the wind is in my favor, but maybe I'll want to go to that stand in a crosswind condition. I might feel I can compromise myself a little bit.''

Keller usually does not hunt one particular stand. To release some of the pressure on any one stand, he uses up to three alternate stands.

Which stand Keller hunts, of course, is determined by a variety of factors. Although there is no ideal hunting situation, there are times and conditions when one stand will be better than another.

"Whichever stand you choose, the No. 1 factor is to approach it undetected," he says. "You've got to think of that fantastic nose that kills us all. The other thing is this: There are some really good hunters out there. They are aware of all these factors, but because they are so aware of everything, they don't give themselves the chance to hunt. That usually results in the comment, 'I saw him, but I never got the shot.'

"Say, for example, you have a buck that is going from point A to point B and he is a 3½- or 4½-year-old deer. If you have a buck that has lived all those years, he will be hunter-wise. If you're a hunter who has everything, that buck is going to be 100 percent wrong for you. You will want that buck to walk into a situation and make himself vulnerable. But the reason the buck is 3½ or 4½ years old is that he doesn't make himself vulnerable. Once in a while a hunter has to go a little bit further. Sometimes he has to go into an area where he will almost be vulnerable to the deer in order to actually get a shot at the animal—especially with a bow and arrow. That is where setting up in a crosswind can come into play. That is an example of splitting the difference. Rather than having it all ideal, sometimes you've got to go a bit further.''

How often Keller hunts one particular stand depends upon the buck, stand selection and activity in nearby areas. But as a general rule, he likes to give a stand three days between hunting sessions. "Let's say I have an area where I can approach undetected and I have a parallel connector—say a fence line connecting two pieces of woods," he says. "If I can get in and out of the stand without disturbing anything, I have a tendency to hunt that spot maybe two days in a row. The farther in I have to go, however, the more I am going to disturb. But I would be lying if I said I never hunted a stand three days in a row.

"Also, if I have a chance-of-a-lifetime buck, I'm going to be more inclined to stay all day," he continues, "because each time I come and go, I disturb the area. An all-day sit doesn't have to be that miserable. If I am going to make a setup like that, I must be very comfortable. That's usually a situation where I will take an older stand together with a second stand. I offset them a little in the same tree, so I can sit on one and put my feet on the other. You can really make yourself comfortable up there. Just be sure to wear a safety belt and bring a bottle to urinate in.''

Going into an all-day stand sitting, according to Keller, isn't usually a problem. He likes to go in very early in the morning and stay in the stand all day. Coming out, however, can be touchy. "I seem to have more trouble jumping deer on the way out in the evening," he says. "If I see I'm going to have a problem going out because there are a lot of deer filtering out, I might say, 'Okay, I put in a good day, I'll sacrifice the evening hunt and sneak out of here before the prime shooting time.' The reason is, I have killed a number of deer from 10:30 to 11 a.m. and from 1:30 to 2:15 p.m.

"There are movement periods during these times, and it's not because of hunting pressure. Those periods of movement have always been there. I know a couple bowhunters who have good luck going in at 9 a.m. and sitting until 2 p.m. Deer just don't sit curled up all day

The height of your tree stand will be determined by a number of factors, including terrain, available shooting lanes at various heights and the amount of background cover that's available.

waiting for the night to feed. Sometimes I'll sit in my tree stand and there will be times of relative quietness. And then there will be an activity period, maybe by the squirrels, that will drive me nuts. I don't think any animal is designed to bed down in the morning and sit in a ball until dark. There are some animals that do that, but definitely not whitetails.''

Keller said one of the most common tree-stand hunting mistakes is to approach the tree-stand site from the same direction every time. He also said that he does not gravitate to a scrape or a phenomenal amount of sign. Instead, he is looking for a spot with a good deer density.

When selecting a spot for a tree stand, Bob Fratzke attempts to choose a stand site where he will be comfortable. ''I'm trying to pick one that has another tree alongside of it about 2 feet away,'' he says. ''I can hang my bow in that tree or lean up against it. Oftentimes, I will find a good comfortable tree, and then try to move the deer to that position using mock scrapes and licking branches.''

Like Keller, Fratzke says the height of his tree stand varies with the terrain, background cover and available shooting lanes. Fratzke tries to get at least 15 feet off the ground.

"Oftentimes, if you go any higher than this, your shooting distances get noticeably shorter because other branches get in your way,'' he says. ''Plus, if I get any higher that steep angle means I will trace too sharp of an arrow angle. That can result in only clipping one lung.''

There is, of course, no universal tree-stand height that's perfect for all bowhunting situations. Wind, terrain, the game being hunted and shot angle must be considered. The key is to get above the game's immediate line of sight and above the understory while still having an accurate shot to the vitals. It won't do you any good to be 18 or 20 feet up with a panoramic view if you can't shoot accurately. Always practice shooting from your selected height at another location. And be sure to check your state's regulations governing tree-stand height limits.

Tree-Stand Safety

Even though tree stands have probably helped improve deer hunter success as much as anything in recent years, hunting from a stand does have disadvantages. An estimated 28 percent of all hunting accidents are related to tree-stand use, according to L.J. Smith of the Hunter Education Association. In fact, the Centers for Disease Control found that tree-stand accidents—according to a Georgia study of hunting injuries—account for 36 percent of hunting accidents! Unless tree-stand safety is practiced, serious falls or other accidents can occur. For example, Bill Martin used a tree stand without an accident for more than 25 years. But, on November 1, this 42-year-old Minnesota bowhunter climbed down from his stand and an 8-foot limb broke from the tree when he grabbed it with his hand. He went over backward and landed on his neck and back.

Martin, then a Master Hunter Safety Instructor with the Minnesota Department of Natural Resources, remained motionless. He knew better than to jump up after such a fall. After more than 30 minutes, he moved his toes, then feet, then legs. He felt pain in his back, but everything, including his hands and arms, still worked.

With the help of his hunting buddy, Martin got back on his feet, climbed up the tree, lowered his bow and tree stand and took out his tree steps. He shouldered his gear and painfully walked 1½ miles back to his pickup truck. Assuming he was only bruised, he drove home and went to bed, thinking he would feel better the next day.

The next morning Bill went to his job as a machinist. By 11 a.m. he was in too much pain, so he went to the hospital. Doctors took a look and told him he had pulled and strained a few muscles. In reality, he had done more.

Martin continued to visit the hospital for treatment of unrelenting pain in his back. Four months after the accident doctors discovered with the aid of a CAT scan that he had broken the scapulas, or shoulder blades, in his back.

Nearly four years after the accident, Martin is still taking medication, still undergoing physical therapy and still suffering from migraine headaches. The total cost for that one fall, which Martin said happened so fast he had no time to react, is staggering. He has missed eight months of work and medical bills total nearly $100,000. Fortunately, he has insurance.

Tree-stand accidents happen fast and even to the most experienced hunters. Hunting from a tree stand can be dangerous. Often, it is the result of carelessness. More often a hunter falls from the tree while going up or coming down.

Most of these accidents can be avoided if hunters follow one simple rule of safety: Wear a safety belt while climbing a tree, while in the stand and when descending the tree.

Many stand manufacturers include a safety belt with their tree stand. All should. If the stand you purchase does not have a safety belt, buy one immediately from a sporting goods store. Don't promise yourself that you will buy one someday. Buy one when you buy your tree stand.

Also, several safeguards should be taken in connection with your tree stands:

● Don't build or use a permanent wooden tree stand. Nails used to build a permanent stand are a danger to someone running a saw. Also, the wood used to construct a stand can rot quickly. Instead, use a portable stand, even if you are going to leave it at the one site, where legal, for an extended period of time.

● Select a live tree that is straight or leans back from where your stand is fastened. A forward slanting tree limits the range of safe movement.

● Guard against putting a stand on a tree that creaks when you shift your weight.

● Make sure your tree stand is in good working condition. You should have the manufacturer replace any worn or missing parts and tighten all nuts each season.

● Always use some type of safety belt to secure yourself while you're in the tree.

● Never climb up or down the tree while carrying your hunting equipment. Instead, use a nylon line to raise and lower equipment after climbing up or down.

● For ease in getting up and down from your stand, use portable, safe climbing blocks or similar non-marring tree steps.

One of the best instructional video tapes available today for safe tree-stand use is "Today's Portable Tree Stands ... Simple Tips on Safety." Trailhawk Tree Stands produced this noncommercial, 16-minute video, which has been approved by the Hunter Education Association and the Wisconsin Department of Natural Resources for use in hunter education programs throughout North America.

This video explicitly details climbing procedures and the proper use of portable tree stands, tree climbers, seat climbers, safety straps and tree ladders. The video should be required viewing for all first-time tree-stand hunters; experienced tree-stand hunters will benefit from this informative video, too.

"This video is urgently needed by sporting goods dealers, retail stores and hunter education programs throughout North America in order to provide an adequate education to hunters on the safe and proper use of tree stands," says Frank Hood, president of Trailhawk Tree Stands.

To support the growing efforts of the Hunter Education Association, Trailhawk Tree Stands makes a financial contribution to the Hunter Education Association for each video tape purchased. (For information, contact Trailhawk Tree Stands, Dept. NAH, 108 Clinton, La Crosse, WI 54603.)

Also, a few remodeling improvements to your portable tree stand can make your hunting efforts more successful. For example, sponge rubber or outdoor carpet secured to your stand allows you to turn around and change your footing noiselessly. In addition, camouflaging your tree stand will better conceal you.

Bowhunters can increase their success rate by practicing at every available opportunity and making adjustments for any shooting variations due to a stand's height and location. Check all directions for branches and obstructions and mark known distances along established shooting lanes.

An excellent source for information is "The Tree Stand Guide," published by the National Bowhunter Education Foundation (NBEF). This 40-page booklet examines most styles of tree stands now on the market, including climbing devices and methods. Instructions for the

All bowhunters should use safety belts when they are up in a tree stand. It doesn't matter how much experience you've had. Accidents can and do happen. Tree stands account for a third of all hunting accidents.

safe, effective use of these products are included, as well as valuable tips on how to be more successful when hunting from a tree stand.

This guide answers the question, "What if you fall?" and provides some good, solid emergency first-aid advice. The booklet is the second in a series of responsibility guides produced by NBEF for hunters. (Contact NBEF Equipment & Supply, Dept. NAH, Rt. 6, Box 199, Murray, KY 42071.)

Another pertinent publication is "Tree Stand Safety," a booklet containing tree-stand safety tips from the NRA. (Contact NRA Sales Department at 1-800-336-7402.)

18

Guided Big-Game Bowhunts

Whether your tree-stand hunting strategies are successful or not, there's no way to set up on game that doesn't live in your hunting arca. To hunt those animals, you must travel to their home territory. Some bowhunters prefer self-guided hunts—planning and coordinating the hunt from home, then attempting to locate particular game once they get to the area. Other bowhunters book guided big-game bowhunts and enlist the expertise of a local guide. Still others opt for a guided hunt the first year and go back without a guide in subsequent years.

Guided hunts should be the experience of a lifetime. They should be the source of stories you share with family and friends. Select the right guide or outfitter and you will spend time with one of the area's best woodsmen and most knowledgeable hunters. You will also have a better opportunity, all else being equal, to bag the big game that you're hunting.

As with any service, however, there are bound to be some lemons—a few guides who should be avoided. Although it's no guarantee, the tips in this chapter should help you avoid these lemons while taking you step by step through the process of selecting a big-game guide. You will learn how to get more than just the "satisfied clients" list from every guide, and how to use the world's largest guide-rating service compiled by NAHC Members. Finally, you will read a story about actual guided hunts.

Detailing Your Dream Hunt

Guided bowhunts cost thousands of dollars. For that price, you should be able to book the type of hunt you dream about—within reason. The first step to booking that hunt is to understand exactly what you want. Before you talk with a guide or start to call a list of references or walk through a sport show collecting brochures, you should outline your dream hunt in detail.

If you are like most bowhunters, you probably already have this hunt figured out. Perhaps you have been daydreaming about a hunt you read about in *North American Hunter* or talked about with a friend. Sit down and put into writing what type of hunt you want.

Answer these questions:

1. What species do I want to hunt?
2. What size animal would I consider a success?
3. Am I looking for a trophy-only hunt?
4. Will I take any respectable animal?
5. Am I willing to take any legal animal?
6. Where will I find the size of animal I want?
7. If I had my druthers when would I hunt?
8. How physically demanding of a hunt do I want?
9. What are my physical limitations?
10. What is most important on the hunt? Bagging an animal o joying being outdoors?

Hunting magazines like *North American Hunter* can be a source of hunt possibilities. Save feature stories that catch your eye or sound like the type of hunt you desire. Read through the ''Hunting Reports'' column that appears in every issue. These reports are submitted by NAHC Members like yourself and are often straight-shooting evaluations of the guides and outfitters. Save any ''Member Shots'' pages that have game or scenery representing your dream hunt. Also, keep a watchful eye out for the NAHC Big Game Registry which is a compilation of the score sheets submitted by NAHC Members on the animals they have harvested with a bow, muzzleloader, rifle and handgun. Hunt location is also given, as well as date of harvest—all useful information.

If you want to harvest a record-book or trophy-class animal, first consult the Pope and Young and Boone and Crockett record books. These books list trophy-class big-game animals harvested with a bow and arrow and with firearms. Another good resource is the *Longhunter Society Big Game Record Book* which features record-book game animals harvested with muzzleloaders.

''Before I even consider outfitters, the first thing I do is zero in on

A guided big-game hunt can pair you up with one of the best woodsmen and most knowledgeable hunters in the area. This guide is glassing the slopes of Colorado's San Juan mountains in search of a trophy-sized elk.

The author (right) utilized a guide's services for a bowhunting trip in South Dakota. The hunt was for trophy pronghorn antelope. The bowhunters used binoculars and spotting scopes to search the terrain.

areas where animals get big," says Chuck Adams. "I can't see any reason for spending my valuable vacation time hunting an area where I don't at least have the off chance of seeing a trophy-sized animal. I'm not a snob about trophy game, but I don't know anybody, even my friends who are meat hunters, who would shoot a small buck beside a big buck. So I research the record books. I look at the entries for the last 10 years. What happened in 1965 doesn't count anymore. There might be a shopping mall where a big buck was killed in 1965. I research the record books and zero in on states and preferably counties that are producing big animals. And if it's provinces of Canada, I do the same thing."

If the size of the animal is not important, decide what is. Perhaps the hunting location is paramount. Or maybe the opportunity to hunt with an outfitter you read about in a book or magazine is paramount. Decide what is most important, then find an area where your dream hunt is possible.

Select A Big-Game Guide

Once you have determined what would comprise your ideal, guided big-game bowhunt, the next step is to research and select your big-game guide. The guide you select will have the greatest impact on the type of hunt you can expect. Also, once you find an area to hunt, your guide will have the greatest impact on whether you will have the opportunity to succeed.

Having decided what you want from your guided hunt, the next step is to locate reputable, recommended guides who offer the hunt you want. If possible, start big and narrow it down. If possible, start with six guides or outfitters.

One of the best ways to come up with these potential guides is to use the world's largest computerized guide and outfitter rating service. As an NAHC Member, you have access to the NAHC's Approved Outfitters and Guides rating service. To receive the coveted "NAHC Approved" status, outfitters must be recommended by at least 75 percent of NAHC Members who hunt with them. These reports are tabulated and compiled in the "NAHC Approved Outfitter & Guides" booklet. That booklet is available free to NAHC members. In addition to listing approved outfitters, the booklet also lists the game species each outfitter specializes in and whether the outfitter guides gun hunters, bowhunters or muzzleloading hunters. The address and telephone number of each recommended outfitter is also included. (For your free copy, contact NAHC Approved Outfitters Booklet, P.O. Box 3401, Minnetonka, MN 55343).

Not only can you access the guides in every state that have been approved by your fellow NAHC Members, but you can also request copies of the actual hunt reports filed on specific outfitters by your fellow Members. By reviewing these reports, you will be able to see what these NAHC Members have to say about quantity of game hunted, quality of game hunted, experience of the guide, competence of other personnel, condition of camp equipment, food and accommodations. You will also be able to find out the length and cost of the hunt. Plus, you will learn if the hunting terrain is unusually tough. You will also find out if the NAHC Member bagged a game animal, whether a gun or bow was used and the time of year. Plus, there is a place for the NAHC Member's name, address and telephone number on the report. You can personally contact the Member to talk over the hunt and the guide's performance.

Though there is a nominal fee for copying and mailing the reports to you, that information is available to you as a benefit of being an NAHC Member. (For more information, contact Hunting Reports, NAHC, P.O. Box 3401, Minnetonka, MN 55343.) And just because an outfitter is not listed in the "NAHC Approved Outfitters & Guides" booklet doesn't mean that the outfitter is not recommended. The NAHC may not have received a sufficient number of hunting reports from NAHC Members on that particular outfitter to determine whether the outfitter should receive the NAHC Approved status.

"Once I zero in on an area I call fish and game departments, look in back of outdoor magazines and talk to taxidermists to find out about outfitters within those areas," Adams says. "And, then, I call the outfitters. I don't work through the mail because outfitters are very busy and the response time is too slow. The first thing I do is quiz them generally about their hunting operation, especially how they hunt. If they're not congenial and don't seem willing to please, I cross them off the list right away. I figure once they have my money it's going to be really downhill if they're not even polite on the telephone."

Adams' next step is to determine whether the prospective guide understands bowhunting. Preferably, he should be a bowhunter himself or he should at least have taken bowhunters out quite a bit in the past. "There are some terrific gun-hunting guides who are not qualified to guide bowhunters," Chuck says. "I unfortunately have been out with a couple of them. If they don't understand bowhunting, it doesn't matter how hard they try. I don't want to be put in the position of training my guide to bowhunt while I'm paying for a hunt Also, I always try to allot enough guided-hunt time for me to get my animal. If the hunt period seems too short to me, I'll steer away from that particular guide. I think a bowhunter needs at least seven solid days for most North American species, and I prefer 10 for most. There are many five- and six-day bowhunts out there, and I found the success rates are lower with those hunts because there is not ample time."

Brochures and pamphlets distributed by guides can be a good source of information initially. Even though they can be a good representation of what you might expect, remember that those publications present the outfitter in the best light possible. The photos will typically showcase the biggest game ever harvested. And the references, if provided, probably will be the most satisfied hunters.

"I request—and I am very adamant about this—a complete list of the outfitter's clients from last year," says Adams. "Then I call those clients or contact them by mail. I don't want the guide's preferred list of four or six or eight people who are probably the ones who were the happiest last year. An outfitter would be silly to give the potential client a list of the soreheads who went out with him. I want that complete list. I want to talk to the soreheads. I want to talk to the people who were not necessarily successful at bagging their animal, as well as those who were successful. Then I am the one who decides whether the outfitter was doing his job properly. I don't want the out-

An experienced guide who knows the terrain and the animals' habits can be a big help when it comes down to tracking game and locating prime hangouts like this wallow. This expertise can work for you for a more enjoyable and successful hunt.

fitter to sway me in a particular position by giving me the good list.''

When reading an outfitter's brochure or talking to the outfitter on the phone, be cautious about hunter-success claims. For example, ''More than 30 percent hunter success on elk!'' doesn't tell you much. Does that 30 percent mean three out of 10 bowhunters bagged elk? Or three out of 10 gun and bowhunters? How many hunters does this figure include? Perhaps the guide only took out three bowhunters for elk last year, and one of them bagged an elk. Perhaps the one elk taken by a bowhunter last year was a cow. Find out whether this hunter success rate is for gun or bowhunters or both. Also, find out whether hunters' success was with taking bulls or cows ... or both.

Another party to contact for information about a guide is the state game departments or the state guides and outfitters associations.

''Once you have it narrowed down to the guides who guide in the area you want to hunt, call the state or provincial fish and game department,'' says Wayne Carlton. ''Ask them about the guide. Is the guide licensed in the state? And have you had any encounters with this particular guide? Usually, the fish and game departments will say whether someone is good or should be avoided. Also, check with the guides and outfitters association in each state.''

If this sounds like I'm encouraging you to be skeptical about a guide, you're right. You should be. At least when you begin sifting through the hundreds who are available. There are few, if any, situations in your life where you will pay somebody $2,000 or $3,000 for one week of work. When that time is over, that's it. You go home. Every year hundreds of hunters go on good, high-quality guided big-game hunts. But every year a handful of hunters book hunts with guides they would rather forget. Do your homework and look with a critical eye to avoid the lemons.

Prepare For The Hunt

On my first guided big-game hunt, my guide was as fit as a marathon runner. Meanwhile, I had sat behind a desk for the past year and occasionally had gone for short hikes after work and on weekends. On the third day of the hunt, my guide spotted a big, wide mule deer about a half-mile away. He tried to hustle us down into a mountain valley and up the opposite side for a possible shot. Halfway up the other side of the valley, however, I was undeniably, unequivocally whipped. I was breathing like a winded horse and my legs felt like Gumby legs—all rubber. About every 50 yards I had to stop and rest.

Of course, by the time we reached the top of the ridge, the monster mule deer was nowhere to be seen. My physical ability limited

Yes, big-game hunts can be physically demanding. Just ask renown bowhunter Chuck Adams, shown scaling a vertical rock face in a quest for mountain game. Be honest with your guide about any physical limitations you might have.

our opportunities for taking game. I did take a respectable 4x4 mule deer on that hunt, but not the big, wide buck I still think about. For now, let's say this: Be honest about your physical condition.

Six months before the season begins visit your family physician for a complete physical. Tell your physician that you will be starting to train for a guided big-game bowhunt and you would like for him to make sure that it's okay for you to get started. The real key to physical fitness is to break into it gradually and do something that is somewhat enjoyable.

For high-country bowhunts, running and biking will help to get leg muscles into shape, as well as improving your cardiovascular system. It's best to work out every other day, with three workouts per week being ideal. The day of relaxation between workouts gives your muscles time to rebuild.

You may also want to spice up your workouts by strapping on a weighted backpack and hiking through hills. This will prepare your back and shoulder muscles. Again, start light; then slowly work up to a heavier pack or a longer hike in the woods. This type of training can be especially easy if you combine it with something like spring scouting or shed-antler hunting.

Equip Yourself For The Hunt

Most guides and outfitters will supply you with a recommended equipment list. Follow it! Your guide or outfitter works in the environment and should know what is required. If the list calls for woolen long-underwear for a spring black-bear hunt, bring it. Snow could be a possibility at the higher elevations.

The other two items I always carry with me—especially on big-game hunts into remote territory—are a survival kit and a day pack filled with those basic essentials.

A survival kit is mandatory. Eventually—no matter how careful and deliberate you are—there will come a time when you will spend an unexpected night in the woods. When that happens, it should be a simple experience to survive. And it will be if you carry a lightweight survival kit. Failing to bring a survival kit could turn an inconvenience into a dangerous situation.

On an elk bowhunt in Colorado, miscommunication with our guide left Wayne Carlton, our cameraman and me stranded at nightfall on the side of a mountain at 9,500 feet. We were nine miles from camp at the end of a long day's hunt that had started at 5 a.m. We were tired, hungry and thirsty. Our guide had left, taking our horses back to camp. Our canteens and coats, of course, were tied onto the

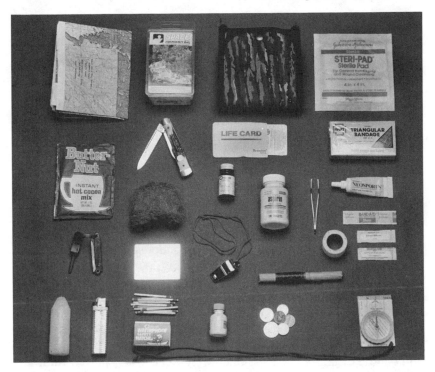

All these items should be a part of a survival kit that stays with you everywhere you go on a hunt. Keep it attached to you, not on the saddle or in your day pack. You may need it when you least expect it.

horses. After a couple minutes of creating new-fangled profanities that we hoped to share later with the guide, we faced the realization that we would be there for the night.

The point of this story is that I got a good night's sleep—reportedly snoring even—because of a little survival kit that I always carry with me. The kit is simple, inexpensive and lightweight. That night it made the difference between a fairly comfortable night and one that could have been a disaster.

My survival kit includes matches, water purification tablets, a space sleeping bag and a snack. That's it. Matches, of course, can provide a source of life-preserving warmth. Water purification tablets can make water safe for drinking, killing giardia which is becoming common in mountain streams. And the space sleeping bag provides dry, emergency shelter under almost any circumstances. All of this fits into a small, zippered plastic bag.

That night was a test of the survival equipment. Because it was successful, I look back on it as an adventure. At no time were we close to having a life-threatening situation, but it could have been bad if we hadn't been prepared or if the weather had taken a turn for the worse. Spending that night on the mountain gave us a chance to compare survival gear.

Among the three of us were a space sleeping bag, a space blanket and a plastic leaf bag. Of the three, the space sleeping bag won hands down. Although the space blanket was big enough for a huddled person to wrap around himself, the space sleeping bag was large enough to spread out and crawl into. Using my boots as a pillow, I was reportedly snoring in 10 minutes. The cameraman with the leaf garbage bag was just plain miserable. It wasn't big enough to crawl into and he was up around 1 a.m. building a fire to stay warm. In fact, the space sleeping bag at one point got too warm, so I ripped a hole in the side to provide circulation and prevent condensation. Because space sleeping bags and blankets are thin and fragile, after one use it's best to spend a few bucks and buy a new one. New ones also pack better.

The second kind of pack to take with you afield is a small one containing the basic essentials you will need that day. Of course, the contents will vary with the type of hunt, but basic items would be a map and compass, knife, sharpening stone, fire-starter kit (matches and candle or an inexpensive butane lighter), water purification tablets and a plastic bag for holding water, binoculars, extra wool socks, extra wool sweater, extra gloves, at least 20 feet of strong rope and some type of high-energy food.

Guided big-game bowhunts can be a ticket to a once-in-a-lifetime hunt. Or they can be a frustrating experience. The key is to do your research. Prepare yourself physically for the hunt. And pack the right gear and equipment.

One of the best guided big-game bowhunts I've been on was hunting for pronghorn antelope in South Dakota. After arriving in Faith, South Dakota, we went to the home of Mel Dutton, the inventor of the Mel Dutton Pronghorn Decoy. He had agreed to guide us on a three-day pronghorn bowhunt into the northwestern corner of the state.

At his home, Mel showed us videotapes of buck antelope coming to the decoys. Using the VCR's pause button, he showed us when to draw and when to sit tight. On the walls were several P&Y pronghorn. He shared with us the hunts for some of those bucks. All had been harvested by Dutton during the past 12 years.

The next morning we drove to the Painter Ranch before sunrise. As the sun crept over the horizon, we began glassing for pronghorn

If you don't think physical conditioning for a hunt is important, a few days in the saddle on an extended hunt in the wide-open terrain of the West will probably change your mind.

bucks. It was mid-September and the rut was in full swing. We carried two pronghorn decoys—one doe and one small buck. When we spotted a respectable-sized buck, the plan was to stalk as close as possible without being detected. Then we would set up the two decoys with the doe in front of the buck. The tail of the doe decoy was in the air, signalling that it was ready to breed. When pronghorn bucks see this union about to take place, they will charge in to challenge and even spar with the buck decoy.

The sun was just above the horizon when a good-sized buck was spotted. Wearing camouflage clothes, we stalked to the nearest rise. Mel set me up behind the doe decoy while he moved in behind the buck decoy. This was because the buck pronghorn's attention would be on the buck decoy—not the doe—allowing me the opportunity to rise up, draw back and take the shot.

In less than five minutes, the buck pronghorn spotted the decoys. He came straight for us, stopping perhaps within 20 yards.

Then he turned parallel to the buck decoy. Remembering Mel's instructions from the night before, I rose to my knees. The pronghorn, catching that movement, trotted away several steps. Still, he was only 30 yards away.

I came to a full draw, settled my pin on the pronghorn, but did not shoot. Before I knew it, the antelope was trotting away, out of range.

Mel shook his head, looked at the grass and smiled. There would be more, he said quickly.

And there were. Throughout that first day we set up on perhaps six pronghorn bucks. Yet, we returned after dark to the restaurant empty-handed. Over supper we talked about each buck that we had set up on, and we talked about the good points and the bad points of the day's hunt. Finally, we talked about what we hoped to do differently the next day.

I had only known Mel for 24 hours, but already I was sure that he knew his stuff and put on a top-quality hunt. The result was a fine mount that looks over my shoulder from my office wall.

19

Trailing, Field Dressing And Caping

Sometimes every piece of the bowhunting puzzle fits perfectly. Scouting, practice, stand selection and camouflage all come together, and you execute a perfect shot. When this happens the result should be a well-deserved smile for the camera and a freezer full of tasty meat. However, one important step has yet to be taken.

Following a blood trail requires common sense, patience and attention to detail. It is not rocket science. How well you follow up your shot determines whether you will experience success or frustration at day's end. And once you've found your game, your field-dressing method determines the meat's flavor and quality. This chapter will show you straightforward strategies to trail and recover big-game animals. It will also take you step by step through the field dressing and caping process.

Modern bowhunting tackle is capable of efficiently harvesting every big-game animal in North America. According to Chuck Adams in *North American Hunter*, "No animal in North America can survive a broadhead through both lungs."

A hunting arrow is designed to efficiently harvest game animals as a result of hemorrhaging. A razor-sharp broadhead delivered to the heart or lungs will often dispatch that animal in less than 60 seconds. That's not much time. However, during those few seconds, a fatally wounded animal can easily cover more than 100 yards. When an animal is hit elsewhere, it can easily take much longer. Gut-shot animals, for example, may take several hours or more to die.

Most bowhunters, unless they mistakenly hit the spine, will have to use their blood-trailing and game-recovery skills. No matter how open the terrain or how good the first shot, never assume you can simply walk over and recover your game.

Successful Trailing Strategies

Successful trailing begins the moment you release your arrow. As you release, continue to concentrate on the aiming point; you should also watch the arrow or fletch as it hits the animal. Listen for the sound of your hit. (Bowhunters often hear a short "punch" sound as the arrow penetrates.) A soggy, slushy-sounding hit often indicates a complete pass-through; an abbreviated, solid punch often indicates the arrow encountered bone. Whether or not you see or hear the result of your shot, watch for a reaction from the animal.

Sometimes, a fatally hit animal will bolt a short distance, then stop and look back at where it was standing. Stay completely quiet. Watch the animal closely. Place another shot in the vitals if possible. Make note of any tree and/or shrub the animal passes. Watch how it runs or walks until you can no longer see it. Then listen for its progress until you can no longer hear it.

When you can no longer see or hear the game, mentally map out what happened and determine the direction the animal was traveling. If you have a compass, take a reading of the direction it was heading. Next, note the exact spot the animal was standing when you shot. Pick out trees, shrubs or landmarks—as many as you can—which the animal passed. If you have a map of the area or a piece of paper, quietly sketch out what happened. Put an "X" on the spot where the animal was standing. Draw the route it traveled and note those landmarks it ran past. Write down the compass bearing. And write a brief note about how the animal reacted to your shot.

Although fatally hit animals never react exactly the same, there are some typical reactions. A well-hit, big-game animal, for instance, usually runs with its tail down. A heart-shot animal may instantly charge off and show no sign of being hit; a gut-shot animal will often hunch its back or jump.

What you do after the shot depends upon the weather, time of day, hunting conditions and shot placement.

Weather and time of day will influence when you should start blood trailing game. Given ideal conditions (no rain and more than one hour of remaining daylight) wait for at least 30 minutes—preferably one hour—after the shot. Why? Because often a well-hit ani-

Once you've scored a hit and successfully trailed the arrowed game, your job is not finished. This chapter focuses on proven game-recovery methods and how to field dress and cape big game.

mal will travel a short distance, then bed down. If you start following the animal too soon or make too much noise you could push the animal even farther into cover. And the farther the animal goes, the more difficult it is to recover.

Under less-than-ideal hunting conditions, you may need to begin blood trailing earlier, risking the chance of pushing your game. For example, rain or snow can quickly wash away or cover up a blood trail. Waiting 30 minutes to an hour under these conditions could leave you with little, if any, blood sign and make trailing impossible. When hunting under these conditions, determine the animal's direction and speed of travel, then search for and pinpoint the point of impact. Better yet, avoid taking a shot under conditions that will quickly cover or wash away any blood trail.

Time of day must also be considered. If you shoot just before dusk, the legal closing, you need to find the blood trail that evening rather than waiting until the next morning. Rain or snow could fall during the night, and unless you have marked the point of impact and at least started to follow the blood trail to determine the animal's direction of travel, you will have little chance of recovering your game.

When you are not familiar with the terrain, exercise caution before wandering through the woods looking for blood sign. (This is especially true in the West where most hunting terrain is rugged and remote.) A lost hunter will hinder rather than help the game recovery effort. On guided big-game hunts, guides often advise that a hunter wait for assistance before following the blood trail. An experienced guide should be familiar with the area and may know the animal's most likely route of travel. If you are required to wait for assistance before blood trailing, make sure you have a good mental image of where the animal was standing when you shot, how it reacted to your shot and which direction it traveled.

Terrain can also influence how soon you follow up your shot. In open country, hunters may want to stalk closer if game goes out of sight, over a pass, around a butte or down into a valley. However, in most cases, bowhunters should avoid following up immediately after the shot. The chance of getting within bow range of a spooked, arrowed animal is slim. If possible, wait 30 minutes before you begin blood trailing.

Finding Point Of Impact

Before you begin blood trailing, tie a fluorescent ribbon on your tree stand, ground blind or a nearby tree. This will serve as an easy reference point when you are following the blood trail and need to

The key to effective trailing is to be patient. You're never sure what you'll find or where you'll find it. Sometimes blood sign will be found on the underside of leaves where it's easily missed.

look back to confirm the direction of travel. It is surprising how difficult it can be to locate your tree stand or ground blind when you're looking at it from a different angle.

The first blood-trailing task is to find the location where the animal was standing when you shot. Mark that location with a piece of toilet paper or flagging tape. Search thoroughly for your arrow. Study all blood and/or hair you find on the ground, arrow shaft, fletch or broadhead. Hair color and blood composition can help you estimate the point of entrance and exit.

Often you can approximate where you hit an animal, based on the blood's color or composition. Bright red blood with bubbles often indicates a lung hit; dark red blood indicates a liver hit. And blood mixed with visceral material often indicates a gut shot. Even if you don't find any blood, do not give up. Game with only an entrance wound may leave little blood sign. Also, game animals with thick layers of fat or lots of hair—especially black bear—leave a limited,

Even minute specks of blood on leaves are important clues when searching for the game that you've shot. Following a blood trail can be a real lesson in "down and dirty" detective work.

most often hard-to-follow blood trail that makes trailing a very slow process.

Once you have thoroughly examined that location, proceed slowly and carefully in the direction the animal traveled. Look for the next sign of blood. Your hunting partner should stay at the last blood sighting while you look for the next blood sign. If working with a hunting guide, your guide may be more experienced at blood trailing and may take the lead. When trailing, do not walk on the blood trail. Stay to one side in case you have to retrace your steps.

If the blood trail is easy to follow, mark it occasionally with flagging tape or toilet paper. (Whatever you use, be sure to pick it up when you are finished trailing.) Walk quietly and slowly.

As you follow a blood trail, try to determine where the blood is in relation to the trail. Blood on both sides of the trail often indicates a pass-through. Also, blood drops hitting the ground often "splatter" or "run" in the direction the animal is moving.

Rediscovering The Blood Trail

If you lose the blood trail, mark the last blood spot with highly visible marker. Look back at the trail formed by your flagging tape or toilet paper. You should be able to determine a general direction of travel. If you can, slowly continue down that line of travel, looking for any blood sign. If there is none, return to the last spot where you found blood.

From the last blood sign, begin working outward in a small, spiraling circle. You may have to get down on your hands and knees to look for any small blood spots.

Blood sign found earlier may help predict where a fatally hit game animal may be located. Typically, well-hit animals travel downhill. Gut-shot animals often head toward water, if available.

If you are still unsuccessful at rediscovering the blood trail, use a product that makes blood appear fluorescent. Sure Sign from Robinson Laboratories—like similar products from other manufacturers —is sprayed on the ground near the last blood sign. If the spray comes in contact with any blood, it will change the dark-colored blood to a fluorescent bright yellow. Not only is this product a great way to find additional blood sign, it is also a boon to those hunters who are color confused and cannot see red blood spots. An estimated 8 percent of all hunters are color confused, according to the late Red Chaplin, who helped direct the study that established Hunter Orange as a hunter's best protective color.

If these techniques prove unsuccessful, check every game trail in

If you have difficulty in following a blood trail because you can't tell if it's blood that you're seeing, there's a product to help you. It causes blood to change to a bright yellow color.

the area. Look carefully on each trail for blood sign.

Because so many big-game animals are active just before dusk, blood trailing after sunset is often unavoidable. If you're in this situation and you know the area well, a Coleman lantern is one of the most valuable tools to use. Light from a Coleman kerosene lantern makes blood spots shine—almost glow—like red emeralds. If you've blood trailed at night with a Coleman lantern, you know about the difference—especially if you've tried blood trailing with a flashlight.

Trailing after dark in almost any area can spell disaster. Trooping through the night into unfamiliar territory may be bold, but it can also leave you lost and tired. Get help, and tell somebody where you will be and when you will return. If possible, consider waiting until morning to resume the blood trail. Of course, if it is warm the animal could easily spoil by morning. However, try to make an educated decision, leaning toward the safety side in making that decision. If you do leave the blood trail until morning, place highly visible markings at each blood spot so the trail will be easy to pick up. Whatever you decide, avoid heading out into unfamiliar territory after dark on your own. Even if you find the animal, you may not be able to pack the animal out of the woods by yourself without becoming lost.

Approaching Downed Game

Always approach downed game with caution. Before charging up to claim your trophy, take a moment to make sure it is dead. Once in a while, you will read about a deer hunter who approached a buck only to discover it was still alive. A wrestling match, although rare, sometimes ensues. Check the animal's eyes. A dead animal's eyes should be open. If they are closed, do not approach. This is especially true when hunting more dangerous game like bear or wild boars. Use caution. Toss a stick at the animal. Some bowhunters poke the animal with a broadhead-tipped arrow to make sure it is dead. If you are in any doubt, aim carefully and fire another arrow into the animal's vitals.

Estimating Live Weight Of Deer

NAHC Members can estimate the weight of their deer in the field by simply taking one easy measurement. According to the Wisconsin Department of Natural Resources, that measurement is the chest circumference. Measure just behind the front legs, then use the accompanying chart to determine the animal's approximate weight.

Chest Size	Live Weight	Field Dressed Weight
(inches)	*(pounds)*	*(pounds)*
35	136	112
36	145	120
37	156	129
38	166	139
39	178	149
40	204	172
41	210	177
42	218	184
43	234	198
44	250	212
45	267	228

Field Dressing Big Game

Field dress your game animal as soon as possible. Some animals, especially those with thick layers of fat and those in mild to warmer climates, can spoil quickly. If you did not recover your broadhead or any part of your arrow shaft, be extremely careful when you field dress the animal. The broadhead or part of the arrow shaft may be inside the body cavity.

Here are three simple steps you can follow to field dress your big-game animal:

1. Place the animal on its back and make an incision just below the sternum. Slip two fingers into this cut, pull the hide up and away from the internal organs, and carefully cut down to and around the sexual organ to the anus. Be careful not to puncture internal organs. Then, go back to the sternum and cut through the abdominal wall, using the same technique from the sternum to the pelvic bone. Again, be careful not to puncture any internal organs.

2. Inside the body cavity, carefully cut around the diaphragm where it connects to the inside of the body cavity. Reach up into the chest, grab the windpipe and pull it toward you. Cut the windpipe as far forward as you can, being careful not to cut yourself. Pull most of the internal organs out of the body cavity.

3. Inside the abdominal cavity, cut around the large intestine. Be careful not to cut the urethra or the intestine. From the outside, cut around the anus and tie it off with a piece of string. From the inside, pull the large intestine and the urethra into the body cavity. Turn the animal on its side and empty all blood and remaining organs.

Some hunters will split the pelvic bone to help cool the hind quarters. Also, many hunters place a stick in the chest cavity to help it cool. These common-sense practices should help keep your game meat from spoiling.

Caping Your Trophy

Trophy game animals are rare. When you harvest a trophy, a shoulder mount can be your reward for years of hard work. It can be a terrific reminder of fond hunting memories.

As I write this, a shoulder mount of my first P&Y animal, a pronghorn, watches over me. Sometimes, I just sit back and look at him and remember. I relive the afternoon when he charged across that South Dakota prairie to challenge my buck decoy. I remember how he licked his nose so he could smell better; it turned glossy black, then faded to flat brown in the warm September breeze. I remember how he twisted his neck to check on his harem of eight does. I remember

Cuts Required For Proper Caping

All you need to do is follow the dotted lines. This diagram shows how the cuts should be made so that you can properly cape your next trophy buck. Your taxidermist will thank you.

this and more because of this shoulder mount.

After field dressing the animal, we began to cape what appeared to be my first potential P&Y trophy. Had it not been for the expertise of Mark Kayser with the South Dakota Department of Tourism, I probably would have botched the cape or worse. Nobody had ever explained the relatively simple process of caping a trophy buck or bull for a shoulder mount. But Mark knew how and helped me complete the task.

How you cape your trophy will determine, in part, the quality of your finished shoulder mount. Here are five simple steps for caping your next trophy buck or bull. This process leaves the delicate task of skinning the head to the taxidermist or your big-game guide.

1. Cut the hide from the base of the sternum straight up to the backbone on both sides. Be sure to start this cut behind the front legs. The finished cut should go completely around the body.

2. Cut around each front leg at armpit level. Then cut from each

armpit cut straight back to the sternum cut.

3. Start at the base of the skull and make a cut on the top of the backbone down to the sternum cut.

4. Starting at the sternum cut, separate the hide from the body by pulling the hide up toward the head. Use a knife as required, but be careful not to puncture or slice the hide.

5. Pull the hide over the skull as far forward as possible. Cut off the skull and cape where the base of the skull and the top of the neck meet. Store cape in a cool place and deliver to your taxidermist as soon as possible.

Successful big-game recovery is a skill requiring patience and persistence. Follow the guidelines set forth in this chapter. When every piece of your bowhunting puzzle fits into place, the result will be a well-deserved smile and a freezer full of tasty meat.

20

Frequently Asked Bowhunting Questions

North American Hunting Club's Bowhunting Advisory Council answers all bowhunting questions for NAHC Members. This free service is provided exclusively for NAHC Members. Since the creation of the BAC in the late-1980s, hundreds of bowhunting questions have been answered. Questions, of course, change with the hunting seasons. Deer season brings out questions about stand selection, scents and camouflage. In the spring, NAHC Members want information about scouting and proven practice strategies. Year after year, however, a handful of bowhunting questions persist. Here, then, are answers to those most commonly asked bowhunting questions.

Question: How much kinetic energy do I need for good penetration on game animals larger than deer?

Answer: It is generally believed that for big game weighing more than 500 pounds, the minimum acceptable kinetic energy is 50 foot-pounds, with 55 to 65 foot-pounds preferred.

To compute kinetic energy a bowhunter must know his arrow velocity (V) and total arrow weight including broadhead (W). A visit to your local archery pro shop will provide these two variables. A chronograph will give your arrow speed; a reloader's scale will show you total arrow weight. Then, just plug these two numbers into the following equation to determine your setup's kinetic energy in foot-pounds:

$$\frac{\text{Velocity x Velocity x Weight}}{450,240} = \text{Kinetic Energy}$$

If, for example, you determine your arrow velocity is 210 feet per second and your total arrow weight is 550 grains, your kinetic energy would compute like this:

$$\frac{210 \times 210 \times 550}{450,240} = \frac{24,255,000}{450,240} = 53.87 \text{ foot-pounds}$$

If your kinetic energy is above the recommended minimum, terrific. If not, follow the advice of your archery pro shop. Increasing draw weight is one of the easiest ways to boost arrow speed and increase your bow's kinetic energy. Of course, if you increase draw weight, be sure to consult the arrow shaft selection chart at the pro shop because you may have to shoot stiffer spined shafts.

Question: I have been hunting with a gun for many years, but now I want to start bowhunting. What archery equipment do I need to get started?

Answer: The best advice is to visit your local archery pro shop. Tell them you want to start bowhunting and would like to purchase the basic gear you need to start shooting. More sophisticated equipment can be purchased once you are comfortable shooting your basic setup. Also, most manufacturers offer bowhunting packages designed for entry-level bowhunters.

The first item you will need is a properly fitted bow that is comfortable to shoot. It may be a few dollars higher at a pro shop than at a discount store that sells toasters, tires, blue jeans and bows. However, you are more likely to receive a properly fitted bow at an archery pro shop than at a mass retail store. Plus, some archery pro shops have tuned bows set up so that you can try them out before you buy.

You will need at least three—possibly four—accessories that mount directly on the bow. First, you will need an arrow rest. The best advice concerning your first arrow rest is the old adage, "keep it simple." The simpler, the better. Many successful, well-known bowhunters shoot a simple Springie or Flipper-type arrow rest. Both are easy to install, effective and inexpensive.

The second item, mounted on the bow, should be a sighting system. Pin sights and crosshair sights are both effective and inexpensive. Once again, keep it simple.

Third is an inexpensive nock which the archery pro shop can install. It identifies the spot where you nock your arrow.

The fourth accessory is a bow-mounted or hip quiver to carry your arrows. A bow-mounted quiver is not required when you first start

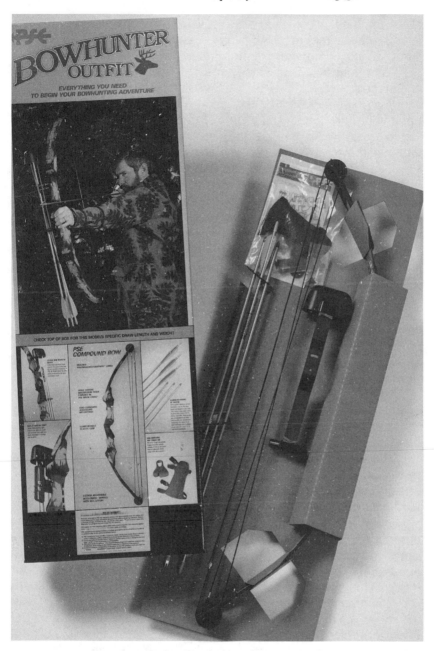

Most manufacturers offer bowhunting starter kits including everything needed to start shooting. This kit includes bow, bow-mounted quiver, two-pin hunting sight, arm guard, finger tab and arrows.

shooting, but it is convenient. However, a hip quiver will work. Plus, keeping the arrows off the bow gives your bow arm time to build up strength and get comfortable holding a bow at full draw.

After your bow is outfitted, you will also need at least six properly sized arrow shafts. Use an arrow-shaft selection chart at your archery pro shop. Basically, the arrow-shaft size you select depends upon your draw length and weight. Most archery pro shops nock and fletch the arrow shafts. Plus, they will cut the arrows to fit your setup and install inserts to accept screw-in field points for target practice.

Two other basic accessories you will want to have are an arm guard and finger tab. The arm guard goes on the forearm of your bow arm, protecting it from the bowstring when you release it. Most likely, you'll only forget this accessory once. The finger tab protects your fingers when you draw back the string and release. Even though you may eventually shoot a mechanical release aid, new shooters should start with a finger tab.

These are the basic bowhunting accessories you will need to start shooting a bow. Once you're comfortable shooting your setup, visit the archery pro shop to buy the broadheads, camouflage clothing, string silencers, stabilizers and any other accessories you desire.

Question: My broadheads do not group the same as my field points. What's the matter with my setup?

Answer: Most bowhunters must adjust their sights when they switch from shooting field points to shooting broadheads. This is because most broadheads are aerodynamically different from a streamlined field point.

You should practice with field points during the off-season to improve shooting form and consistency. Then, long before the hunting season opens, start shooting broadheads and adjust your sights accordingly.

Shoot your broadheads before you go hunting. Not only will your broadheads group differently than your field points, but even the same make and model broadheads from the same manufacturer may not group exactly the same. For example, I often shoot 125-grain Rocky Mountain Razors, because I find them to be aerodynamically stable and very effective on big game. However, once in a great while I'll shoot one that just won't group as tightly as the others. That one I will straighten or throw. Even though this seldom happens, I want to have 100 percent confidence in my equipment. Blade heads should be sharpened after each shot. Shooting broadheads with dull blades is only asking for trouble when you're going after big-game animals.

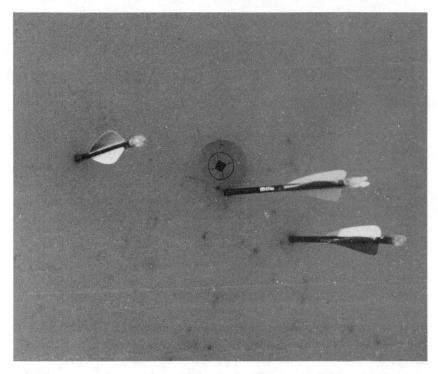

Attention to detail and practice are important elements of successful bowhunting. If, in practice shooting with broadheads, you get a shot group like this one, you know that some fine tuning is required.

More than likely the broadhead will only penetrate a short distance or bounce off.

In addition to finding out how each broadhead flies, there is another psychological advantage in shooting broadheads during practice. When I shoot field points, I know I'm practicing —even if I'm shooting into a 3-D target. However, when I shoot broadhead-tipped arrows, my concentration climbs measurably. The more I practice with broadheads, the more confidence I have in my hunting setup.

Another way to boost familiarity and confidence in broadheads is to find out which broadhead shoots best with which arrow shaft. Many bowhunters number their arrow shafts. They will shoot these numbered shafts with field points, and weed out any that do not group with the others. Then they switch to broadheads on the remaining shafts and repeat the process. The result is true-flying, broadhead-tipped arrows in which the bowhunter will have complete confidence.

Judging distances from a tree stand can be deceptive. Distances should be measured on the ground. Then practice shooting at targets from a stand and measure the distances.

Question: How much should I compensate in sighting when shooting from a tree stand?

Answer: With the number of people who hunt from a tree stand, it is surprising how few practice shooting from an elevated position. The best answer to this question is to climb into a tree stand or elevated platform and see how your setup performs. Basically, two factors must be considered when shooting at a downward angle: actual distance and shot angle.

When looking at an object from an elevated position, it appears to be farther away than it actually is. The solution is to measure distances to trees or landmarks from the base of your tree stand, not from your elevated position. Choose several landmarks, then pace off the distance or use a rangefinding device. From your tree stand you can use these landmarks as a reference to approximate the distance to other objects or to the animal itself.

On level ground, a broadside shot behind the front shoulder will hit both lungs. From an elevated stand a shot behind that front shoulder may only strike through one lung before exiting the chest area because of the steep angle of the arrow's path. (Successful bowhunters consider the shot angle when they place their stands.) Practice shooting from a tree stand at 3-D targets, if possible, to better understand the effects of distance and shot angle. Take advantage of local archery clubs that have an elevated setup or 3-D competitions.

Question: Which is better for harvesting and tracking a game animal, a shot that completely passes through or one that stays in the animal?

Answer: The most important factor for any bow shot is to put a razor-sharp broadhead into the heart and lung area. That is the paramount consideration. Regardless of whether you have the "pass through" or "keep the arrow in the animal" view, the determining factor for every bow shot must be a clear shot into the vitals.

The argument most often heard for keeping the arrow in the animal is that when the animal runs, the broadhead continues to cut tissue, keeping the wound channel open. This sounds beneficial. However, a razor-sharp broadhead shot into the vitals—whether it passes through or stays in the animal—inflicts sufficient damage to cleanly and efficiently dispatch a big-game animal.

Personally, I prefer a pass-through shot. It is much easier to blood-trail an animal with two holes rather than one. With animals having thick skin or layers of fat, such as black bear or wild pigs, this is especially true; however, it helps even with deer and elk.

In Nova Scotia, I followed an arrowed whitetail. On a 15-yard shot from a tree stand, the arrow entered high behind the front shoulder, cut efficiently through the vitals and exited low in front of the opposite front shoulder. The animal traveled about 100 yards before piling up.

An inspection of the entrance and exit wounds disclosed that little, if any, blood had been lost through the high entrance wound. The low exit wound obviously was the source of perhaps all the blood loss. If the arrow had stayed in the animal rather than passing through it, there would have been only the high entrance wound, and we would have found little, if any, blood.

Of course, the exception to blood-trailing a complete pass-through shot is when hunting turkeys. Most bowhunters will attach a special arrow penetration suppressor to their broadhead so they won't shoot completely through a gobbler. The arrow in a turkey will keep it on the ground during those few seconds before the bird dies.

Question: Besides increasing arrow speed, how can I reduce or eliminate the chance of a deer jumping my string?

Answer: There are two solutions: equipment and hunting style.

One of the easiest ways to keep a deer from jumping the string is to quiet your release. This can be done by adding silencers to the bowstring, and mohair, moleskin or rubber to all metal parts on and around your arrow rest; a short stabilizer, specially designed for bow-

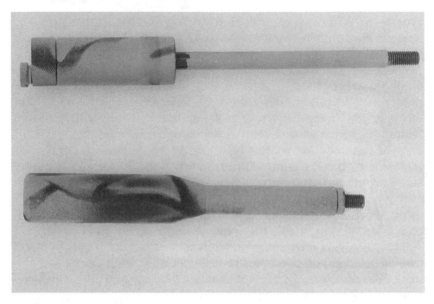

A stabilizer will help you silence your hunting outfit. Stabilizers like those shown above will quiet your release and tighten your groups by adding weight to balance the outfit.

hunters, also helps. Be sure your overdraw, arrow rest and quiver are securely fastened.

A second option is to alter your hunting location and/or the time of your release. An alert deer—one expecting danger—is more apt to jump the string than one quietly browsing or moving from feeding area to bedding area.

Try to find a set-up location where deer feel safe and more relaxed. Once a deer comes within range, wait until it relaxes before you shoot. Waiting for the animal's head to go down or its suspicion to subside will lessen the chance of it jumping the string.

Question: I would like to hunt with a crossbow. What is the best crossbow setup on the market?

Answer: It's virtually impossible to name the best crossbow and arrow setup. Many high-quality, effective crossbows are available.

Ask to see the line of crossbows at your local archery pro shop. Manufacturers like Horton, Precision Shooting Equipment (PSE), Bear and Barnett—to name a few—are known for their quality equipment. Also, most crossbow catalogs include an arrow-shaft selection chart. You should be able to reference this chart at your local archery dealer.

If you're disabled, another potential source of information is David Sullivan of Alabama Handicapped Sportsmen. Any disabled NAHC Members needing information about crossbows may contact him. (David's address is Alabama Handicapped Sportsmen, 44 Huntington Place, Northport, AL 35476.)

Question: I have bowhunted whitetails for several years and have taken a few deer. However, I have not taken what I would consider a trophy buck. What am I doing wrong? I spend time scouting and know the area well.

Answer: Bowhunting legend Myles Keller says one of the most common bowhunting mistakes is hunting areas that have relatively few deer. He says bowhunters must hunt undisturbed areas if they want to use their hunting knowledge and consistently be successful. You should follow Myles Keller's advice and avoid areas with considerable hunting pressure.

Find the place where the big bucks hang out, is the advice of the experts. It may take some searching, but the rewards can be great. A buck like this one is worth the effort.

To determine if any big bucks are left in your hunting area, hunt for shed antlers in the spring. First, of course, make sure it is legal in your state and the hunting area.

Locating shed antlers will put you ahead of other deer hunters; you will know which animals made it through the hunting season and which, perhaps, did not. You'll also know what bucks have wandered into the area.

The best time to search for shed antlers is early in the spring. Look in bedding areas, feeding areas and along trails. Larger-racked bucks typically shed their antlers earlier than smaller bucks. Persistent shed-antler hunters sometimes find both sides of a buck's rack. That gives them a specific buck to hunt during the fall.

Year-round scouting is often the most common factor that separates the consistently successful hunters from those who are occasionally successful. Shed-antler hunting is a great excuse to get out in the spring.

Question: How much do weather conditions, temperature and elevation affect arrow flight. I've heard that at higher elevations the air is thinner and you will shoot higher than normal. Is this true?

Answer: Based upon the hunting and shooting I have done at higher elevations, I've not found that elevation makes a significant difference in point of impact. Of course, I haven't done extensive testing on this, but I carried an altimeter with me on a Colorado elk hunt at altitudes reaching as high as 11,200 feet. I did not notice any significant change in point of impact despite an elevation difference of 10,500 feet from where I usually hunt.

Regarding the potential impact of temperatures on a hunting setup: Last fall I bagged a whitetail after a blizzard that dropped 3 feet of snow. After the blizzard, real temperatures dropped to 10 degrees below zero. The confirmed windchill factor was 40 degrees below zero. That's cold! If any conditions were going to impact the performance of my hunting bow, I would have suspected that it would have happened right then.

I had been sitting in a tree stand for nearly three hours and I had not drawn the bow for at least that long. Yet, when a white-tailed buck walked out in front of my stand at 20 yards, that bow performed without a hitch. That gave me a renewed sense of confidence in modern bows and arrows. The fact that a wheel or an axle or a string didn't freeze up or crack or break is testimony to the quality of bowhunting gear that is available today.

Sometimes camouflaged garments aren't enough. This bow-mounted blind effectively conceals the hunter's face and hands as well as the drawing motion. This blind weighs only 3½ ounces.

Now that I think about it, we were bringing our bows into the hotel room at night. That means that they were being moved through an 80-degree temperature range—from 70 degrees in the hotel room to 10 degrees below zero outside.

A testing ground in the other direction—extreme heat—is the Pete Shepley Desert Shootout held in Tucson, Arizona. At that tournament—which features Olympic champions and the world's top target archers—temperatures can easily climb above 100 degrees. I never heard a hunter say his sights were off because of the heat or warmer weather. It seems most modern bowhunting tackle is impervious to any type of hunting conditions.

Question: The closest I can get to big game out West is about 50 yards. How can I cut down that distance? Or should I rig my setup to shoot at targets 50 yards away? I've tried hunting in my bare feet and with socks. However, I can't get any closer. So, I plan to increase my range to 50 yards. Do you think penetration will be sufficient at 50 yards?

Answer: I do not recommend shooting at any game animal 50 yards away regardless of your bow's setup.

At 50 yards, arrow trajectory is terrible and point of impact changes significantly in one or two yards. Nobody I know can accurately estimate whether an object is 48 or 50 yards away, unless they

Ground blinds can be highly effective, particularly in areas where there may be few trees. Here, the author moves into position to take a shot after having been concealed by the blind.

have measured that distance. And even the latest rangefinders have an accuracy range of plus or minus one yard at 50 yards.

In addition to unsatisfactory trajectory at that range, the shooter also must be concerned about an arrow's diminishing kinetic energy. Will your arrow have sufficient kinetic energy at 50 yards to completely penetrate a mature mule deer buck? What if your broadhead hits a part of the shoulder? Do not shoot at this range. It's not worth the risk.

Instead, change your hunting technique. If you now glass and stalk mule deer, try hunting from a blind. Take the time to pattern the deer, then conceal yourself with brush or camouflage netting along well-traveled routes.

If you can't pinpoint a heavily traveled route, use a portable camouflaged blind. On open Western prairies—where it can be dry and the cover sparse—bowhunters use ground blinds or portable blinds to get within bow range of big-game animals.

Question: I have hunted white-tailed deer for several years. Next season I would like to hunt black bears. It is legal to hunt black bears over bait in our state. What should I know about bowhunting black bears?

Answer: Black bears are the second most common big-game species for NAHC Members, the first is the white-tailed deer. The black bear is a natural transition species for many deer hunters.

In many states and provinces, the most common hunting technique is over a bait station. Most states have regulations governing stations, including what you can use as bait and when you can start baiting. Read state game regulations carefully for the area in which the hunt will take place before beginning your hunt.

Most bowhunters prefer to hunt black bears from a tree stand. This gets them up above the understory so they can see the bear approaching.

Black bears can be extremely quiet—even bears weighing 300 and 400 pounds can slip through the woods without making a sound. Don't be surprised if you suddenly see a black bear on your bait without knowing how he got there.

Sows with cubs and very large black bears will sometimes break branches or snap small trees while heading into a bait station. When you hear that, be prepared. It probably will be either a big bruin or a sow with cubs. Of course, it is illegal to shoot a sow with cubs. If a sow and her cubs come into the bait station, It's best to shout or at least clear your throat to let them know that you are there. Having a black bear sow and her cubs around you can be dangerous. Try to let them know you are there without panicking them. You especially don't want a cub climbing in a tree near your stand and getting the mother suspicious or defensive.

Sometimes the bear will circle downwind from the bait station before approaching it. With their extraordinary sense of smell, many bruins will circle downwind of even a fermenting bait pile to see if anybody else—human being or bear—is at the bait station.

Whatever bowhunting tackle you use for whitetails should also work well for medium-sized black bear, even though they do have thicker hides, more hair and thicker layers of fat than whitetails. If you have a deep-penetrating setup, use it on black bears. If you have a mediocre setup barely sufficient for whitetails, buy a new bow or boost your present setup's arrow velocity and kinetic energy before hunting black bear.

Don't forget for a moment that black bear can be dangerous. They can also leave notoriously poor blood trails. Experienced black-bear hunters strive for a complete pass-through shot. Two holes result in a better blood trail.

Some black-bear bowhunters use string trackers attached to the front of their bows. The string is tied to the broadhead end of the arrow shaft and spooled on a special tube-like container that fits into the bow-stabilizer bushing. When the arrow is shot, it pulls the string with it. Therefore, if the arrow penetrates a black bear, the end of the string will, too. You can watch the string go out as the arrowed bear heads away from the bait station. When it stops, the bear has either died or bedded down. However, sometimes the string can come off the arrow or the arrow pulls out of the bear.

Approach an arrowed black bear with caution. Even though black bears are not usually regarded as extremely dangerous, they can be. Occasionally, you may run into a rogue bear that does not have an instilled fear of man. Approach a downed bear as you would any downed wild animal.

Question: What is the difference between a 50- and 65-percent let-off bow?

Answer: If you have a 60-pound, draw-weight bow with a 65-percent let-off and an identical 60-pound, draw-weight bow with a 50 percent let-off, the 65 percent let-off bow will reach peak weight sooner, but must be drawn at that peak weight over a longer distance. Its holding weight, however, is only 21 pounds, and stores more potential energy with faster arrow speeds.

The 50 percent let-off bow will be smoother to draw. The increase in draw weight should be gradual. A 50 percent let-off bow with a holding weight of 30 pounds stores less energy than the 65 percent bow and probably will yield slightly slower arrows.

21

Bowhunting: Building
For The Future

Modern bowhunting's first 80 years have been a period of tremendous change and growth. Even those in the 1920s who saw potential for using the bow again to hunt would be surprised at the look and capability of the modern compound bow. Perhaps the next 80 years will have even more dramatic changes in bowhunting. Bowhunting's future is shaped by you, today's bowhunter.

The groundwork that has been laid by the Pope and Young Club, bowhunting organizations and state and national archery associations is a solid base for the sport's future growth.

Bowhunting's Pope And Young Club

The Pope and Young Club was created in 1961 to record big-game trophies taken with a bow and arrow. The club hoped to bolster the image of bowhunting as a viable hunting sport and game management tool. "The Pope and Young Club was originally conceived because bowhunting was considered by most state game agencies as a rather silly, ineffective way of hunting big game," says former P&Y president and NAHC Bowhunting Advisory Council member Jim Dougherty. "Simply stated, the club's purpose was to prove otherwise by fostering the principles of trophy (selective) hunting under the rules of fair chase, promoting the welfare and conservation of North American big game and their habitat and presenting bowhunting as an honest, healthy, outdoor recreation. That the concept succeeded resoundingly is a credit to the men who founded it, notably Glenn St. Charles and bowhunters themselves.''

It was St. Charles, P&Y president from 1967 to 1972, who guided P&Y through its formative years. St. Charles, in *Brief History Of The Pope and Young Club*, wrote, ''Modern bowhunting as we know it today began many years before when Will 'Chief' Compton and Saxon Pope introduced bowhunting to Art Young. The adventures of this trio paved the way for others to come, who struggled to prove that bowhunting was indeed a manly art. The upward fight was slow. The public, gun hunters and conservation departments throughout the country had to be assured that bowhunting was good conservation and a factor in game management.''

By all measures, the P&Y Club succeeded. In 1962, P&Y recognized just 227 big-game animals, and had a total of 25 regular members and 67 associate members. By 1992, 30 years later, P&Y recognized nearly 19,000 big-game animals and boasted 100 regular members, more than 2,000 associate members and about 100 senior members. As Dougherty says, '' ... from a struggling organization that barely possessed the proverbial pot, it evolved into a self-sufficient, financially sound organization that generates many thousands of dollars for valuable conservation projects.''

Conservation projects received more than $60,000 in 1991, according to P&Y President G. Fred Asbel. ''And that's from an organization that had a total budget of just $150,000. Our group tends to be people who are interested in trophy hunting to a degree and people who are interested in the protection of bowhunting and ethical hunting. We're finding a tremendous number of people are joining our organization because they believe in what we are doing, because they believe in conservation.''

Asbel says P&Y will continue to record trophy big-game animals; however, the organization also faces the challenges that have threatened bowhunting opportunities. In particular, the threat comes from the anti-hunters and animal-rights fanatics. ''We're getting much more involved in efforts to promote and protect bowhunting,'' Asbel says.

Dougherty agrees. ''Hunting, in any form, will continue to draw increased fire from elements of a plastic-wrap society completely out of touch with the reality of nature or any honest concept of life itself,'' he says. ''The club's mission is larger today than simply just protecting bowhunting. We walk hand-in-hand with other organizations equally dedicated to the universal cause of environmental protection, perpetuation of our wildlife ... and protection for game and

Much has been done to create and preserve hunting opportunities for future generations. However, a lot more needs to be done. To hunt trophy animals in the future, good game management is necessary.

As bowhunting's largest record-keeping organization, the Pope and Young Club recognizes nearly 19,000 big-game trophy animals. These record-book mule deer were displayed at the club's biennial convention.

non-game species alike. We continue to put energies and dollars where others offer celebrated bodies, mouths and occasional tax deductible checks. There is no question we are right. But it's getting tougher to defend.''

P&Y Membership Requirements

From the beginning, P&Y has maintained high standards and strict requirements for membership. Addressing high membership requirements during the creation of the club, St. Charles is quoted as saying, "We must realize that perhaps our membership under this requirement will not fill up as fast and probably our objectives will not be reached as quickly, such as publishing a book. We can, however, begin work on a modest book and start small. I believe in the overall picture. We will be glad that we maintained a high level for membership requirements.''

Those requirements include:

Associate Member. An unlimited number of people can be associate members of P&Y. However, to qualify, a bowhunter must have taken at least one adult North American big-game animal with a bow and must submit a P&Y application form.

Regular Member. Regular membership in P&Y is limited to 100 members. To qualify for regular membership, a bowhunter must have harvested at least three different adult North American animals with a bow. At least one of these three animals must be listed in the P&Y record book *Bowhunting Big Game Of North America*. Once an associate member is eligible for regular membership, he or she must submit an application. Then, when a regular member position is available, the associate with the most seniority is given the opportunity to become a regular member.

Senior Member. Being a senior member is the most advanced stage of membership in P&Y. Regular members who have taken four adult species of North American big-game animals with a bow, have three of those animals listed in the P&Y record book and have held regular-member status for five years automatically become senior members.

Entering A Trophy For Consideration
There are four simple steps NAHC Members must take to have a bow-killed, big-game animal entered in the P&Y record book, according to Glen Hisey, P&Y records chairperson.

1. Allow the skull or trophy rack to dry for 60 days at room temperature and at room humidity.

2. Have the trophy measured by an official P&Y or Boone & Crockett scorer. (A list of official scorers in your state is available from P&Y, Dept. NAH, P.O. Box 548, Chatfield, MN 55923.)

3. Provided the animal's score meets the minimum requirement for inclusion in the record book, submit the official score sheet with a signed fair-chase affidavit, a photo of the trophy and the required entry fee to P&Y.

4. The club will then examine the score sheet and story of the hunt. Provided everything is in order, the club will officially recognize your trophy and send you a certificate suitable for framing. Your trophy will then be included in the next edition of the P&Y record book.

P&Y recognizes the following big-game species categories: Alaska brown bear, black bear, grizzly bear, polar bear, bison, barren ground caribou, mountain caribou, Quebec-Labrador caribou, woodland caribou, cougar, Colombian black-tailed deer, Sitka black-tailed

In order for a top 10 animal to qualify as a record, it must be panel measured. Other animals making the record book must be scored by a P&Y official scorer.

deer, Coues' deer, mule deer, white-tailed deer, Roosevelt elk, Yellowstone elk, Alaska-Yukon moose, Canada moose, Shiras moose, muskox, pronghorn, Rocky Mountain goat, bighorn sheep, Dall sheep, desert sheep and Stone sheep. The four non-typical species include the non-typical whitetail, mule deer, Coues' deer and Yellowstone elk.

Potential new world-record animals and the top animals in each species must be panel-measured to be officially recognized. Panel measurement is completed at the biennial P&Y convention. Trophies are panel-measured in time for a formal presentation of the top three finishers and honorable mentions in each category.

P&Y's Top Honor: The Ishi Award

The Ishi Award is the highest honor given by the P&Y Club. It can only be awarded at most once every two years, and then only when a hands-down, head-turning trophy animal has been taken. It is named after Ishi, the Yana Indian who stepped out of the Stone Age and into modern society in 1911. Some past Ishi award winners include Del Austin, 1965 non-typical whitetail; Mel Johnson, 1969 typical whitetail; Ray Alt, 1971 Bighorn sheep; Art Kragness, 1973 barren ground caribou; Michael Cusack, 1975 Alaska-Yukon moose; B.G. Shurtleff, 1979 Columbia blacktail; Ray Cox, 1981 black bear; Jerry James, 1983 cougar; Bill Barcus, 1985 mule deer; Gary Laya, 1987 dall sheep; James Ludvigson, 1989 non-typical Yellowstone elk; James Decker, 1991 non-typical Columbia blacktail.

Pope And Young Club's Future

"From a small group of dedicated individuals who only wanted a chance, the Pope and Young Club has flourished to a solid entity that stands at the highest plateau in cherishing and protecting the ethics of conservation, good sportsmanship (and) sound game management..." says Dougherty, who first joined the club in the early 1960s and became a senior member in 1973. "Given that, I'm extremely honored and pleased to have been involved."

The Future Of Bowhunting

At a local archery range a short time ago, a teenage girl was shooting a recurve, aided by a man who appeared to be her father. The girl wore a bigger smile than anybody else. While the rest of us "serious" shooters looked sternly at our targets and tried even harder to tighten our already tight groups, she was tickled just to be shooting a bow. She even asked her father if she could go bowhunting.

Such an experience prompts one to consider what the future may hold for this young would-be bowhunter. And, inevitably, that leads to an attempt to foresee what the future might hold for all bowhunters, particularly in light of apparent population encroachment into traditional hunting areas.

Will bows be significantly different 10 or 20 years from now? Will we still enjoy long archery seasons, and ample big-game hunting opportunities? How effective will the anti-hunters and animal-rights activists be at trying to abolish bowhunting? Will bowhunters everywhere respond to their public challenge and stand up and fight for the tradition of bowhunting?

During the past 80 years bowhunting has been lifted from the primitive age of Ishi, the Yana Indian, into the modern age by the likes of Saxon Pope, Art Young, Fred Bear, Chuck Adams and many, many others. When Ishi walked out of those California woods, there was, quite possibly, just one bowhunter in North America—Ishi. To-

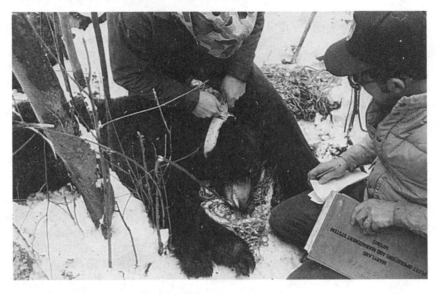

Money from sportsmen and sportswomen provide a major portion of research funding for restoration and preservation of game-animal species. Monitoring the activities of bears is an example of this type of research.

day, there are 3 million who enjoy the sport of bowhunting!

Bowhunting And Game Animals

Hunters are among North America's true conservationists. Bowhunters, together with all other hunters in the United States, have contributed to the restoration of wildlife and wildlife habitat through a voluntary tax on most sporting equipment. Through the Federal Aid in Wildlife Restoration Act, bowhunters pay an 11 percent tax on certain archery equipment. That money is distributed to states to better manage wildlife. Since this program and one for fishermen were started more than 60 years ago, an estimated $12 billion in hunter dollars have gone to rebuild and restore both game and non-game species to abundance.

Here are some of the most notable wildlife restoration efforts that have been accomplished with funds from sportsmen:

● In 1920, there were only 500,000 white-tailed deer in North America. Today, there are more than 14,000,000.

● In 1920, there were only 100,000 elk in the United States. Today, there are more than 500,000.

● In 1920, there were fewer than 25,000 pronghorn antelope in the United States. Today, there are an estimated 750,000. (An increase of 3,000 percent!) Habitat restoration projects also benefit non-game animals. According to most barometers, North American big-game populations should remain healthy for years to come.

Bowhunting Equipment's Future

In 1911, the year Ishi appeared, bows and arrows were made from wood and broadheads were chipped from rocks. Bowhunting had not progressed beyond that level of technology for thousands of years. Since 1911, however, technology and creative thinkers have carried bowhunting into the modern age. In 1946, the first aluminum arrow was introduced; in the 1960s, the first compound; in 1983, the cam-operated bow.

Today, bows and arrows are manufactured from high-tech, space-age materials. And modern bowhunting tackle can cleanly and efficiently harvest every big-game animal in North America, as well as wild game of other continents. Chuck Adams has taken all 27 recognized North American species—the first bowhunter in history to accomplish such a feat. That's something only a handful of firearms hunters can claim.

Where can the modern compound bow go after that heady accomplishment? What else do we want a bow and arrow to do? Of course, the answer came in the form of super straight aluminum arrows and space-age carbon arrows. And each spring at archery pro shops, bow-

Machined risers such as this one from PSE are rapidly replacing magnesium risers in a number of top-quality bows. Machined from a single block of aluminum, these risers are very durable.

Sportsmen have united to fend off attacks by anti-hunting groups that are opposed to bowhunting and gun hunting of game animals. Hunters' messages reflect conservationism and emphasize that America's wildlife is thriving.

hunters can find better designed, more efficient bows.

Modern technology allows bow manufacturers to design and build bows that, with some limitations, do exactly what bowhunters want. Want a super fast bow? It's available—just be sure to shoot a mechanical release. Want an accurate, smooth, forgiving bow? That's available, too—just be sure to accurately estimate the distance to the target to accommodate for the trajectory. In general, bows and bowhunting tackle are well-designed—hunters just need to learn to use them properly.

Detecting The Anti-Hunting Movement

If anyone should understand the predator/prey relationship, it should be hunters. Anti-hunters are stalking bowhunters like predators. They are gradually building momentum in efforts to keep hunters from enjoying the sport. And they will succeed unless hunters take the time to stand up and fight.

In order to protect their sport, bowhunters must be willing to defend it from attacks by all anti-hunting groups. Otherwise, bowhunters could well lose the right to hunt by default.

Game that ignore impending danger usually end up dead. Bow-hunting, unless bowhunters rally together, could end up the same way. When bowhunters make an effort to band together and give up a Saturday to promote and protect bowhunting, they usually succeed. The key is to band together and present to laymen the positive aspects of hunting.

There is no denying the fact that bowhunters are independent. One of the greatest joys in life is to hike into the woods, climb into the tree stand and hunt—alone. Bowhunters enjoy the solitude, the quiet, the one-on-one challenge.

If bowhunters rally together on important issues, your children and their children should be able to enjoy this great sport for a life-time. The first line of defense against any anti-hunting attack is at the local level. Keep abreast of what is happening in your area and help protect the sport of bowhunting by belonging to a local, regional or state archery organization. These organizations are aware of impending legislation and can alert their members.

New AMO Arrow Weight Standards

In response to growing safety and product liability concerns, Archery Manufacturers Organization (AMO) has set minimum arrow weight standards at 6 grains for every pound of peak maximum draw force. Shooting arrows lighter than the 6-grain standard - in the interest of higher arrow speeds - could over stress archery equipment, causing damage to the gear and/or injury to the shooter.

The International Bowhunting Organization (IBO) adopted identical arrow weight guidelines last year. The National Field Archery Association (NFAA) set its arrow weight standards by requiring that all arrows be equipped with 100-grain point assemblies. Both groups put the bow draw weight maximum at 80 pounds.

Using the Minimum Recommended Arrow Weight Chart

- Select the column that describes the type of bow you shoot
- Move down that column to locate your Actual Peak Bow Weight
- Move horizontally across that row to your "AMO Draw Length" column
- The box at that location contains the minimum total arrow weight recommended for your equipment

1. Arrow weight includes all arrow components - shaft, insert, point, fletching and nock.
2. Based on: • 360 Grain Arrow • 30" Draw Length • 60# Peak Weight • Speed Cam

SE=Stored Energy • ESE=Energy Storage Efficiency • BH=Brace Height • PDF=Peak Draw Force

Actual Peak Bow Weight In Lbs.				AMO Recommended Minimum Arrow Weights (Grains)								
Recurve	Round Wheel	Energy Wheel	Speed Cam	25"	26"	27"	28"	29"	30"	31"	32"	33"
$\frac{SE}{PDF}=.95$	$\frac{SE}{PDF}=1.04$	$\frac{SE}{PDF}=1.20$	$\frac{SE}{PDF}=1.3+$									
ESE =62 BH =9.5	ESE=65.6 BH =9.0	ESE=71.3 BH =8.0	ESE=75.1 BH .=7.0									
33	32	29	27	150	150	150	150	150	150	150	150	150
34-41	33-38	30-35	28-32	150	150	150	150	150	150	150	151	165
42-46	39-43	36-39	33-36	150	150	150	150	150	163	179	195	211
47-52	44-49	40-44	37-41	150	150	150	167	185	203	222	240	258
53-58	50-54	45-49	42-46	150	163	183	203	224	244	264	285	305
59-63	55-60	50-54	47-50	172	195	217	240	262	284	307	329	352
64-69	61-64	55-59	51-55	202	227	251	276	300	325	350	374	399
70-75	65-71	60-64	56-60	232	259	286	312	339	365	392	419	445
76-81	72-76	65-70	61-65	262	291	320	348	377	406	435	463	492
82-86	77-81	71-74	66-69	292	323	354	385	416	446	477	508	539
87-92	82-87	75-79	70-74	322	355	388	421	454	487	520	553	586
93-99	88-94	80-85	75-80	352	387	422	457	492	532	581	629	676

Arrow Shaft Selection Chart

A/C/C for Bowhunting: Carbon (graphite) arrows may be used for hunting if special precautions are taken. See dealer or Easton information with each set of A/C/C shafts.

Bow Weight Table

Broadhead or Field Point Weight Only. Point weight (grains): 75 = 65-85, 100 = 90-110, 125 = 115-135, 150 = 140-160.

RECURVE BOW — BOW WEIGHT¹ (LBS)				COMPOUND — Round Wheel				COMPOUND — Energy Wheel				COMPOUND — Speed Cam			
75	100	125	150	75	100	125	150	75	100	125	150	75	100	125	150
35 to 40	32 to 37	29 to 34	26 to 31	45 to 50	42 to 47	39 to 44	36 to 41	40 to 45	37 to 42	34 to 39	31 to 36	35 to 40	32 to 37	29 to 34	26 to 31
40 to 45	37 to 42	34 to 39	31 to 36	50 to 55	47 to 52	44 to 49	41 to 46	45 to 50	42 to 47	39 to 44	36 to 41	40 to 45	37 to 42	34 to 39	31 to 36
45 to 50	42 to 47	39 to 44	36 to 41	55 to 60	52 to 57	49 to 54	46 to 51	50 to 55	47 to 52	44 to 49	41 to 46	45 to 50	42 to 47	39 to 44	36 to 41
50 to 55	47 to 52	44 to 49	41 to 46	60 to 65	57 to 62	54 to 59	51 to 56	55 to 60	52 to 57	49 to 54	46 to 51	50 to 55	47 to 52	44 to 49	41 to 46
55 to 60	52 to 57	49 to 54	46 to 51	65 to 70	62 to 67	59 to 64	56 to 61	60 to 65	57 to 62	54 to 59	51 to 56	55 to 60	52 to 57	49 to 54	46 to 51
60 to 65	57 to 62	54 to 59	51 to 56	70 to 76	67 to 73	64 to 70	61 to 67	65 to 70	62 to 67	59 to 64	56 to 61	60 to 65	57 to 62	54 to 59	51 to 56
65 to 70	62 to 67	59 to 64	56 to 61	76 to 82	73 to 79	70 to 76	67 to 73	70 to 76	67 to 73	64 to 70	61 to 67	65 to 70	62 to 67	59 to 64	56 to 61
70 to 76	67 to 73	64 to 70	61 to 67	82 to 88	79 to 85	76 to 82	73 to 79	76 to 82	73 to 79	70 to 76	67 to 73	70 to 76	67 to 73	64 to 70	61 to 67
76 to 82	73 to 79	70 to 76	67 to 73	88 to 94	85 to 91	82 to 88	79 to 85	82 to 88	79 to 85	76 to 82	73 to 79	76 to 82	73 to 79	70 to 76	67 to 73
82 to 88	79 to 85	76 to 82	73 to 79	94 to 100	91 to 97	88 to 94	85 to 91	88 to 94	85 to 91	82 to 88	79 to 85	82 to 88	79 to 85	76 to 82	73 to 79
88 to 94	85 to 91	82 to 88	79 to 85	100 to 106	97 to 103	94 to 100	91 to 97	94 to 100	91 to 97	88 to 94	85 to 91	88 to 94	85 to 91	82 to 88	79 to 85
94 to 100	91 to 97	88 to 94	85 to 91	106 to 112	103 to 109	100 to 106	97 to 103	100 to 106	97 to 103	94 to 100	91 to 97	94 to 100	91 to 97	88 to 94	85 to 91

Shaft Size Reference (Shaft Size / Shaft Model / Shaft Weight)

23" (22½"–23½")			24" (23½"–24½")			25" (24½"–25½")		
Shaft Size	Shaft Model	Shaft Weight	Shaft Size	Shaft Model	Shaft Weight	Shaft Size	Shaft Model	Shaft Weight
			1813	75	189	1913	75	209 A
						1816	75, E	232 B
						3L-04	A/C/C	173
1813	75	181	1913	75	200 A	2012	75	198 A
			1816	75, E	223 B	1913	75	209 B
			3L-04	A/C/C	167	1816	75, E	232 C
						3-04	A/C/C	180
1913	75	192 A	2012	75	190 A	2013	75	225 A
1816	75, E	213 B	1913	75	200 B	1916	75, E	251 A
3L-04	A/C/C	160	1816	75, E	223 C	3-18	A/C/C	186
			3-04	A/C/C	173			
2012	75	182 A	2013	75	216 A	2112	75	209 A
1913	75	192 B	1916	75, E	241 A	2013	75	225 B
1816	75, E	213 C	3L-18	A/C/C	179	1916	75, E	251 B
3-04	A/C/C	166				3-18	A/C/C	186
2013	75	207 A	2112	75	200 A	2112	75	209 C
1916	75, E	231 A	2013	75	216 B	2113	75	233 B
3L-18	A/C/C	172	1916	75, E	241 B	2016	S, 75	264 A
			3-18	A/C/C	187	3-18	A/C/C	195
2112	75	192 A	2112	75	200 C	2212	75	219 B
2013	75	207 B	2113	75	223 B	2114	S, 75	247 B
1916	75, E	231 B	1916	S, 75	253 A	2016	S, 75	264 C
3L-18	A/C/C	172	3-18	A/C/C	187	2115	75	269 B
						2018	S, 75, E	307 A
						3-28	A/C/C	203
2112	75	192 C	2114	S, 75	237 B	2212	75	219 C
2113	75	214 B	2016	S, 75	253 C	2213	S, 75	246 A
2016	S, 75	243 A	2115	75	259 B	2114	S, 75	247 C
3-18	A/C/C	180	2018	S, 75, E	295 A	2115	75	269 B
			3-28	A/C/C	194	2018	S, 75, E	307 B
						3-28	A/C/C	203
2212	75	201 B	2212	75	210 C	2312	75	235 B
2114	S, 75	227 B	2213	S, 75	236 A	2213	S, 75	246 C
2016	S, 75	243 C	2114	S, 75	237 C	2215	75	267 B
2115	75	248 A	2115	75	259 B	2117	S, 75, E	301 A
2018	S, 75, E	282 A	2018	S, 75, E	295 B	3-39	A/C/C	210
3-28	A/C/C	186	3-28	A/C/C	194			
2212	75	201 C	2312	75	225 B	2312	75	235 C
2213	S, 75	226 A	2213	S, 75	236 C	2314	S, 75	266 C
2114	S, 75	227 C	2215	75	256 B	2215	75	267 C
2115	75	248 B	2117	S, 75, E	289 A	2216	S, 75	301 A
2018	S, 75, E	282 B	3-39	A/C/C	202	3-49	A/C/C	217
3-28	A/C/C	186						
2312	75	216 B	2312	75	225 C	2413	S, 75	260 A
2213	75	245 B	2314	S, 75	250 A	2315	75	292 A
2117	S, 75, E	277 A	2215	75	256 C	2219	S, 75, E	344 A
3-39	A/C/C	193	2117	S, 75, E	289 B	3-49	A/C/C	217
			2216	75	329 B			
			3-49	A/C/C	208			
2312	75	216 C	2413	S, 75	244 A	2512	75	255 A
2314	S, 75	244 B	2315	75	268 B	2413	S, 75	260 B
2315	75	268 A	2219	S, 75	329 A	2315	75	292 B
2216	S, 75	277 B	3-60	A/C/C	222	2219	S, 75, E	344 B
2219	S, 75, E	314 A				3-60	A/C/C	231
3-49	A/C/C	200						
2413	S, 75	239 A	2512	75	245 A	2512	75	255 A
2314	S, 75	244 B	2413	S, 75	250 B	2315	75	292 B
2315	75	268 A	2315	75	280 B			
2216	S, 75	277 B	2219	S, 75	329 B			
2219	S, 75, E	314 A	3-60	A/C/C	222			
3-49	A/C/C	200						

FOR BOW WEIGHTS HEAVIER THAN INDICATED ON THE CHART: From your arrow length column, move to the right one column (1" longer shaft) for each 6 lbs. your bow is heavier than the maximum weights shown. FOR MECHANICAL RELEASES: From your bow weight row, you could move 1-2 rows lighter (1-2 rows up).

¹ Actual or Calculated Peak Bow Weight

The chart indicates that more than one shaft size may shoot well from your bow. **Shaft sizes in bold type are the most widely used aluminum sizes,** but you may decide to shoot a lighter shaft for speed, or a heavier shaft for greater penetration. Also, large variations in bow efficiency, type of wheels or cams, bow length, string material and release type may require special bow tuning or a shaft size change to accommodate these variations.

"Shaft Size" column—indicates suggested shaft sizes.

The "Shaft Model" column—designates arrow model:
"S" = XX78 Super Slam shafts (7178 alloy)
"75" = XX75 Camo Hunter, PermaGraphics™, Autumn Orange, GameGetter II® and GameGetter® shafts (7075 alloy)
"E" = Eagle® Hunter shafts (6061 alloy)
"A/C/C" = Aluminum/Carbon/Competition shafts

EASTON HUNTING SHAFT SELECTION CHART

This shaft selection chart was set up using • Modern recurve bows • High-performance, 50-65% let-off compound bows over 43" with steel or Fast Flite® cables • Fast Flite® string • Finger release. If your equipment varies from the above, see *A Guide to Bowhunting with Easton Arrow Shafts* for more information.

CORRECT HUNTING ARROW LENGTH — YOUR DRAW LENGTH PLUS 1" CLEARANCE

25½"- 26" -26½"			26½"- 27" -27½"			27½"- 28" -28½"			28½"- 29" -29½"		
Shaft Size	Shaft Model	Shaft Weight	Shaft Size	Shaft Model	Shaft Weight	Shaft Size	Shaft Model	Shaft Weight	Shaft Size	Shaft Model	Shaft Weight
2012 1913 1816 3-04	75 75 75, E A/C/C	206 A 217 B 241 C 187	2013 1916 3L-18	75 75, E A/C/C	243 A 271 A 201	2112 2013 1916 3L-18	75 75 75, E A/C/C	234 A 252 B 281 B 209	2112 2113 2016 3-18	75 75 S, 75 A/C/C	242 C 270 B 306 A 226
2013 1916 3L-18	75 75, E A/C/C	234 A 261 A 194	2112 2013 1916 3L-18	75 75 75, E A/C/C	225 A 243 B 271 B 201	2112 2113 2016 3-18	75 75 S, 75 A/C/C	234 C 260 B 296 A 219	2212 2114 2016 2115 2018 3-28	75 S, 75 S. 75 75 S, 75, E A/C/C	254 B 286 B 306 C 312 A 356 A 235
2112 2013 1916 3L-18	75 75 75, E A/C/C	217 A 234 B 261 B 194	2112 2113 2016 3-18	75 75 S, 75 A/C/C	225 C 251 B 285 A 211	2212 2114 2016 2115 2018 3-28	75 S, 75 S. 75 75 S, 75, E A/C/C	245 B 276 B 296 C 302 A 344 A 227	2212 2213 2114 2115 2018 3-28	75 S, 75 S. 75 75 S, 75, E A/C/C	254 C 285 A 286 C 312 B 356 B 235
2112 2113 2016 3-18	75 75 S, 75 A/C/C	217 C 242 B 275 A 203	2212 2114 2016 2115 2018 3-28	75 S, 75 S. 75 75 S, 75, E A/C/C	236 B 266 B 285 C 291 A 332 A 219	2212 2213 2114 2115 2018 3-28	75 S, 75 S. 75 75 S, 75, E A/C/C	245 C 275 A 276 C 302 B 344 B 227	2312 2213 2215 2117 3-39	75 S. 75 75 S, 75, E A/C/C	272 B 285 C 309 B 349 A 244
2212 2114 2016 2115 2018 3-28	75 S, 75 S. 75 75 S, 75, E A/C/C	228 B 256 B 275 C 280 A 319 A 211	2212 2213 2114 2115 2018 3-28	75 S, 75 S. 75 75 S, 75, E A/C/C	236 C 265 A 266 C 291 B 332 B 219	2312 2213 2215 2117 3-39	75 S. 75 75 S, 75, E A/C/C	263 B 275 C 299 B 337 A 235	2312 2314 2215 2117 2216 3-49	75 S, 75 75 S. 75. E S, 75 A/C/C	272 C 309 A 309 C 349 B 349 A 251
2212 2213 2114 2115 2018 3-28	75 S, 75 S. 75 75 S, 75, E A/C/C	228 C 256 A 256 C 280 B 319 B 211	2312 2213 2215 2117 3-39	75 S. 75 75 S, 75, E A/C/C	254 B 265 C 288 B 325 A 227	2312 2314 2215 2117 2216 3-49	75 S, 75 75 S. 75. E S, 75 A/C/C	263 C 298 A 299 C 337 B 337 A 242	2413 2314 2315 2216 2219 3-49	S, 75 S. 75 75 S. 75 S. 75. E A/C/C	302 A 309 B 338 A 349 B 399 A 251
2312 2213 2215 2117 3-39	75 S. 75 75 S, 75, E A/C/C	244 B 256 C 277 B 313 A 219	2312 2314 2215 2117 2216 3-49	75 S, 75 75 S, 75, E S, 75 A/C/C	254 C 287 A 288 C 325 B 325 A 234	2413 2314 2315 2216 2219 3-49	S, 75 S. 75 75 S. 75 S. 75. E A/C/C	291 A 298 B 327 A 337 B 386 A 242	2512 2413 2315 2219 3-60	75 S. 75 75 S, 75, E A/C/C	295 A 302 B 338 B 399 B 268
2312 2314 2215 2117 2216 3-49	75 S, 75 75 S, 75, E S, 75 A/C/C	244 C 277 A 277 C 313 B 313 A 225	2413 2314 2315 2216 2219 3-49	S, 75 S. 75 75 S. 75 S. 75. E A/C/C	281 A 287 B 315 A 325 B 372 A 234	2512 2413 2315 2216 3-60	75 S. 75 75 S, 75, E A/C/C	285 A 291 B 327 B 386 B 259	2512 2315 2219 3-60	75 75 S. 75. E A/C/C	295 A 338 B 399 B 268
2413 2314 2315 2216 2219 3-49	S, 75 S. 75 75 S. 75 S. 75, E A/C/C	270 A 277 B 303 A 313 B 358 A 225	2512 2413 2315 2219 3-60	75 S. 75 75 S, 75, E A/C/C	275 A 281 B 313 B 372 B 250	2512 2315 2219 3-60	75 75 S. 75. E A/C/C	285 A 327 B 386 B 259	2512 2514 2317 3-71	75 S, 75 S, 75 A/C/C	295 B 329 A 385 A 283
2512 2413 2315 2219 3-60	75 S. 75 75 S, 75, E A/C/C	265 A 270 B 303 B 358 B 240	2512 2315 2219 3-60	75 75 S. 75. E A/C/C	275 A 315 B 372 B 250	2512 2514 2317 3-71	75 S, 75 S, 75 A/C/C	285 B 317 A 371 A 273	2514 2317 2419 3-71	S, 75 S, 75 75 A/C/C	329 B 385 B 422 A 283
2512 2315 2219 3-60	75 75 S. 75. E A/C/C	265 A 303 B 358 B 240	2512 2514 2317 3-71	75 S, 75 S, 75 A/C/C	275 B 306 A 358 A 263	2514 2317 2419 3-71	S, 75 S, 75 75 A/C/C	317 B 371 B 407 A 273	2514 2317 2419 3-71	S. 75 S. 75 75 A/C/C	329 B 385 B 422 A 283
2512 2514 2317 3-71	75 S, 75 S, 75 A/C/C	265 B 295 A 345 A 254	2514 2317 2419 3-71	S, 75 S, 75 75 A/C/C	306 B 358 B 393 A 263	2514 2317 2419 3-71	S. 75 S. 75 75 A/C/C	317 B 371 B 407 A 273	2419	75	422

29½"- 30" -30½"			30½"- 31" -31½"			31½"- 32" -32½"			32½"- 33" -33½"		
Shaft Size	Shaft Model	Shaft Weight	Shaft Size	Shaft Model	Shaft Weight	Shaft Size	Shaft Model	Shaft Weight	Shaft Size	Shaft Model	Shaft Weight
2212 2114 2016 2115 2018 3-28	75 S, 75 S. 75 75 S, 75, E A/C/C	263 B 296 B 317 C 323 A 368 A 243	2212 2213 2114 2115 2018 3-28	75 S, 75 S. 75 75 S, 75, E A/C/C	271C 305 A 306 C 334 B 381 B 251	2312 2213 2215 2117 3-39	75 S. 75 75 S, 75, E A/C/C	301 B 315 C 341 B 385 A 209	2312 2314 2215 2117 2216 3-49	75 S, 75 75 S, 75, E S, 75 A/C/C	310 C 351 A 352 C 397 B 397 A 286
2212 2213 2114 2115 2018 3-28	75 S, 75 S. 75 75 S, 75, E A/C/C	263 C 295 A 296 C 323 B 368 B 243	2312 2213 2215 2117 3-39	75 S. 75 75 S, 75, E A/C/C	291 B 305 C 331 B 373 A 261	2312 2314 2215 2117 2216 3-49	75 S, 75 75 S. 75, E S, 75 A/C/C	301 C 341 A 341 C 385 B 385 A 277	2413 2314 2315 2216 2219 3-49	S, 75 S, 75 75 S, 75 S. 75, E A/C/C	343 A 351 B 385 A 397 B 454 A 286
2312 2213 2215 2117 3-39	75 S. 75 75 S, 75, E A/C/C	282 B 295 C 320 B 361 A 252	2312 2314 2215 2117 2216 3-49	75 S, 75 75 S. 75. E S, 75 A/C/C	291 C 330 A 331 C 373 B 373 A 268	2413 2314 2315 2216 2219 3-49	S, 75 S, 75 75 S. 75 S. 75, E A/C/C	333 A 341 B 373 A 385 B 441 A 277	2512 2413 2315 2219 3-60	75 S, 75 75 S, 75, E A/C/C	336 A 343 B 385 B 454 B 305
2312 2314 2215 2117 2216 3-49	75 S, 75 75 S. 75. E S, 75 A/C/C	282 C 319 A 320 C 361 B 361 A 260	2413 2314 2315 2216 2219 3-49	S, 75 S. 75 75 S. 75 S. 75. E A/C/C	322 A 330 B 362 A 373 B 427 A 268	2512 2413 2315 2219 3-60	75 S. 75 75 S, 75, E A/C/C	326 A 333 B 373 B 441 B 296	2512 2315 2219 3-60	75 75 S, 75, E A/C/C	336 A 385 B 454 B 305
2413 2314 2315 2216 2219 3-49	S, 75 S, 75 75 S, 75 S. 75. E A/C/C	312 A 319 B 350 A 361 B 413 A 260	2512 2413 2315 2219 3-60	75 S. 75 75 S, 75, E A/C/C	316 A 322 B 362 B 427 B 287	2512 2315 2219 3-60	75 75 S. 75. E A/C/C	326 A 373 B 441 B 296	2512 2514 2317 3-71	75 S, 75 S, 75 A/C/C	336 B 374 A 438 A 322
2512 2413 2315 2219 3-60	75 S. 75 75 S, 75, E A/C/C	305 A 312 B 350 B 413 B 277	2512 2315 2219 3-60	75 75 S. 75. E A/C/C	316 A 362 B 427 B 287	2512 2514 2317 3-71	75 S, 75 S, 75 A/C/C	326 B 363 A 424 A 312	2514 2317 2419 3-71	S, 75 S, 75 75 A/C/C	374 B 438 B 480 A 322
2512 2315 2219 3-60	75 75 S. 75. E A/C/C	305 A 350 B 413 B 277	2512 2514 2317 3-71	75 S, 75 S, 75 A/C/C	316 B 351 A 411 A 302	2514 2317 2419 3-71	S, 75 S, 75 75 A/C/C	383 B 424 B 466 A 312	2514 2317 2419 3-71	S, 75 S, 75 75 A/C/C	374 B 438 B 480 A 322
2512 2514 2317 3-71	75 S, 75 S, 75 A/C/C	305 B 340 A 398 A 293	2514 2317 2419 3-71	S, 75 S, 75 75 A/C/C	351 B 411 B 451 A 302	2514 2317 2419 3-71	S. 75 S, 75 75 A/C/C	363 B 424 B 466 A 312	2419	75	480
2514 2317 2419 3-71	S, 75 S, 75 75 A/C/C	340 B 398 B 437 A 293	2514 2317 2419 3-71	S. 75 S. 75 75 A/C/C	351 B 411 B 451 A 302	2419	75	466			
2514 2317 2419 3-71	S. 75 S. 75 75 A/C/C	340 B 398 B 437 A 293	2419	75	451						
2419	75	437									

If you shoot one of the sizes listed below with an aluminum RPS insert, add to your point weight the extra weight indicated to compensate for these tapered shoulder, heavier inserts. Use this total weight as your point weight when using this chart. •2314 add 20 gr. •2312, 2315, 2317, 2413, 2419 add 25 gr. •2512 add 40 gr. •2514 add 35 gr.

WARNING: OVER-STRESSING COMPOUND BOWS BY USING ARROWS LIGHTER THAN AMO RECOMMENDATION MAY CAUSE DAMAGE TO THE BOW AND POSSIBLE INJURY TO THE SHOOTER.
AMO compound bow manufacturers have issued a warning: Total arrow weight (shaft weight [shown on Easton chart] plus weight of point, insert [if used] and fletching plus nock [usually 35 grains]) should be greater than 6 grains per pound of peak bow weight for a 60# compound bow and 30" draw length. • Bow weights lighter than 60# and draw lengths shorter than 30" can use arrows lighter than 6 grains/lb. peak bow weight. • Bow weights heavier than 60# and draw lengths longer than 30" should use arrows heavier than 6 grains/lb. peak bow weight.

FOR ARROW LENGTHS LONGER THAN 33": From your bow weight row, move down one row in the 33" column for each inch your arrow is longer than 33".
FOR ARROW LENGTHS SHORTER THAN 23": From your bow weight row, move up one row in the 23" column for each inch your arrow is shorter than 23".

Rev. 12/91

EASTON's highest performance aluminum hunting shaft, the Super Slam XX78 designed by Chuck Adams, is designated by the letter "S" in the "Shaft Model" column.

The "Shaft Weight" column—indicates shaft weight only. To determine total arrow weight, add the weights of the shaft, point, insert, nock and fletching. Where two aluminum shaft models are shown for one size, the weight listed is for XX75. Letter codes A-C listed to the right of shaft weight indicate the relative stiffness of each aluminum shaft within that "Shaft Size" box ("A" being the stiffest, "B" less stiff, etc.).

Although Easton has attempted to consider most variations of equipment, there are other style and equipment variables that could require shaft sizes other than the ones suggested. In these cases, you'll need to experiment and use stiffer or weaker spine shafts to fit your situation.

AFC's Comparison Chart

V-Max, Carbon Camo, Max II, Exacta	X7	Aluminum XX75	
2100	1916	1916	1917
	2041	2013	2014
2200		2016	2018
	2115	2114	2115
2300	2117	2117	2213
	2213	2216	
2400		2217	2219
		2317	2413
2540	N/A	N/A	

Beman's One-Step Arrow Conversion

Aluminum Shaft	Carbon Shaft
XX75: 1916, 2013, 2014	= Beman Hunter: 30/50
XX75: 1917, 2016, 2114	= Beman Hunter: 40/60
XX75: 2018, 2115, 2213	= Beman Hunter: 50/70
XX75: 2117, 2215, 2314	= Beman Hunter: 60/80
XX75: 2216, 2217, 2413	= Beman Hunter: 70/90
XX75: 2219, 2315, 2317	= Beman Hunter: 80/100

Determining Adjusted Bow Weight

Answer each question		#1 Peak draw force up to 59,9Lbs	#2 Peak draw force over 60,0Lbs	Write correct figure here (plus or minus)
	Measured peak draw force	___	___	=
1	High energy Cam	+8	+10	
	Round wheel	0	0	=
	Modified Cam	+6	+7	
2	65% let-off	-3	-4	
	50% let-off	0	0	=
	35% let-off	+2	+3	
3	Beman Light Adapter +80 grains Field Point or 100 grains Glue-In Point	-5	-6	
	Beman Light Adapter +100 grains Field Point or 125 grains Glue-In Point	-3	-4	
	Beman Standard Adapter +100 grains Field Point	-2	-3	=
	Beman Standard Adapter +125 grains Field Point or 150 grains Glue-In Point.	0	0	
	Beman Standard Adapter +145 grains Field Point	+3	+4	
4	Arrow length 25.9" or less	-3	-4	=
	Arrow length 26.0" or more	+3	+4	
5	Fast Flight	+4	+5	=
	Dacron string	0	0	
6	Finger release	+3	+4	=
	Release aid	0	0	
	Add/Subtract determine adjusted bow weight calculation			=

North American Bowhunting Organizations

If you don't already belong to a state archery association, join one today. The following are state and local bowhunting organizations throughout North America:

Alabama
Bowhunters of Alabama
Dept. NAH
Route 13, Box 401
Jasper, AL 35501

Alaska
Alaska Bowhunters Association
Dept. NAH
P.O. Box 190629
Anchorage, AK 99519

Arizona
Arizona Bowhunters Association
Dept. NAH
P.O. Box 2033
Glendale, AZ 85311

Arkansas
Arkansas Bowhunters Association
Dept. NAH
P.O. Box 9902
Little Rock, AR 72219

California
California Bowhunters/Archery Association
Dept. NAH
P.O. Box 5162
Whittier, CA 90607

Colorado
Colorado Bowhunters Association
Dept. NAH
P.O. Box 24250
Denver, CO 80224

Connecticut
United Bowhunters of Connecticut
Dept. NAH
10 Jewett Street
Ansonia, CT 06401

Delaware
Delaware Bowhunter Education Program
Dept. NAH
Road #1, Box 209
Fredrica, DE 19946

Florida
Florida Bowhunters Council
Dept. NAH
3311 West San Jose Street
Tampa, FL 33629

Georgia
Georgia Bowhunters Association
Dept. NAH
1651 Lakeview Circle
Gainesville, GA 30501

Hawaii
Hawaii Bowhunters Association
Dept. NAH
P.O. Box 362
Honolulu, HI 96725

Idaho
Idaho State Bowhunters
Dept. NAH
P.O. Box 1462
Idaho Falls, ID 83403

Illinois
Illinois Bowhunters Association
Dept. NAH
15962 South Ellis
South Holland, IL 60473

Indiana
Indiana Bowhunters Association
Dept. NAH
10833 E. Coffey Dr.
Columbus, IN 47203

Iowa
Iowa Bowhunters Association
Dept. NAH
Box 872
Waterloo, IA 50704

Kansas
Kansas Bowhunters Association
Dept. NAH
Route 5, Box 1700
Manhattan, KS 66502

Kentucky
Kentucky Bowhunters Association
Dept. NAH
P.O. Box 1425
Henderson, KY 42420

Louisiana
Louisiana Field Archery Association
Dept. NAH
14113 Rampart Court
Baton Rouge, LA 70810

Maine
Maine Bowhunters Society
Dept. NAH
9 Parkview Road
Winham, ME 04062

Traditional Bowhunters of Maine
Dept. NAH
Carvella Road
Mapleton, ME 04757

Maryland
Maryland Bowhunters Society
Dept. NAH
5905 Walker Mill Rd.
Capitol Heights, MD 20743

Massachusetts
Massachusetts Bowhunter Association
Dept. NAH
45 Main Street Suite C-3
Wareham, MA 02571

Michigan
Michigan Bowhunters Association
Dept. NAH
3460 West 13th
Cadillac, MI 49601

Minnesota
Minnesota Bowhunters, Incorporated
Dept. NAH
Box 567
Bryon, MN 55920

Minnesota State Archery Association
Dept. NAH
620 N. Washington
St. Peter, MN 56082

Mississippi
Mississippi Bowhunters Association
Dept. NAH
P.O. Box 7923
Jackson, MS 39284

Missouri
United Bowhunters of Missouri
Dept. NAH
P.O. Box 9885
Kansas City, MO 64134

Montana
Montana Bowhunters Association
Dept. NAH
Box 1119
Malta, MT 59538

Nebraska
Nebraska Bowhunters Association
Dept. NAH
P.O. Box 210
Fairbury, NE 68352

Nevada
Nevada Bowhunters Association
Dept. NAH
5150 Ambrose Drive
Reno, NV 89509

New Hampshire
Granite State Bowhunters
Dept. NAH
24 Pinnacle Street
Hooksett, NH 03106

New Jersey
United Bowhunters of New Jersey
Dept. NAH
Old Stagecoach Turn
Vincetown, NJ 08088

New Mexico
United Bowhunters of New Mexico
Dept. NAH
P.O. Box 20298
Albuquerque, NM 87154-0298

New York
New York Field Archers & Bowhunters,
Incorporated
Dept. NAH
2329 Highland Fruit Farm Road
Lyons, NY 14489

North Carolina
North Carolina Bowhunters Association
Dept. NAH
Route 4, Box 91
Morgantown, NC 28655

North Dakota
North Dakota Bowhunters Association
Dept. NAH
Box 206
Surrey, ND 58585

Ohio
Ohio Bowhunters Association
Dept. NAH
288 Southwood Avenue
Columbia, OH 43207

Oklahoma
Oklahoma Bowhunters Council
Dept. NAH
Route 2, Box 282 B
Jones, OK 73049

Ontario
Ontario Bowhunters Association
Dept. NAH
Box 561
Lucan, Ontario M7A 1W3

Oregon
Oregon Bowhunters
Dept. NAH
86154 Drummond Avenue
Eugene, OR 97404

Pennsylvania
United Bowhunters of Pennsylvania
Dept. NAH
Box 576
Bryn Athyn, PA 19009

Rhode Island
United Bowhunters of Rhode Island
Dept. NAH
136 Scott St.
South Attleboro, MA 02703

South Carolina
South Carolina Bowhunters Association
Dept. NAH
608 Saddlebrook Lane
Hopkins SC 29061

South Dakota
South Dakota Bowhunters, Incorporated
Dept. NAH
908 Mulberry
Yankton, SD 57078

Tennessee
Tennessee Archery Association
Dept. NAH
Route 3, Box 623-A
Dandridge, TN 37725

Texas
Lone Star Bowhunters Association
Dept. NAH
Route 1, Box 104 West
Mission, TX 78572

Utah
Utah Bowmen's Association
Dept. NAH
425 East 400 North
Lindon, UT 84042

Vermont
Vermont Bowmen, Incorporated
Dept. NAH
R.R. D6 Sandhill Road
Milton, VT 05468

Virginia
Virginia Bowhunters Association
Dept. NAH
Route 1, Box 358-A
Keezletown, VA 22832

Washington
Washington State Bowhunters
Dept. NAH
13028 S.E. 237th Street
Kent, WA 98031

West Virginia
West Virginia Bowhunters Association
Dept. NAH
P.O. Box 481
Fairmont, WV 26555

Wisconsin
Wisconsin Bowhunters
Dept. NAH
P.O. Box 240
Clintonville, WI 54929

Wyoming
Bowhunters of Wyoming
Dept. NAH
P.O. Box 126
Dayton, WY 82836

Index

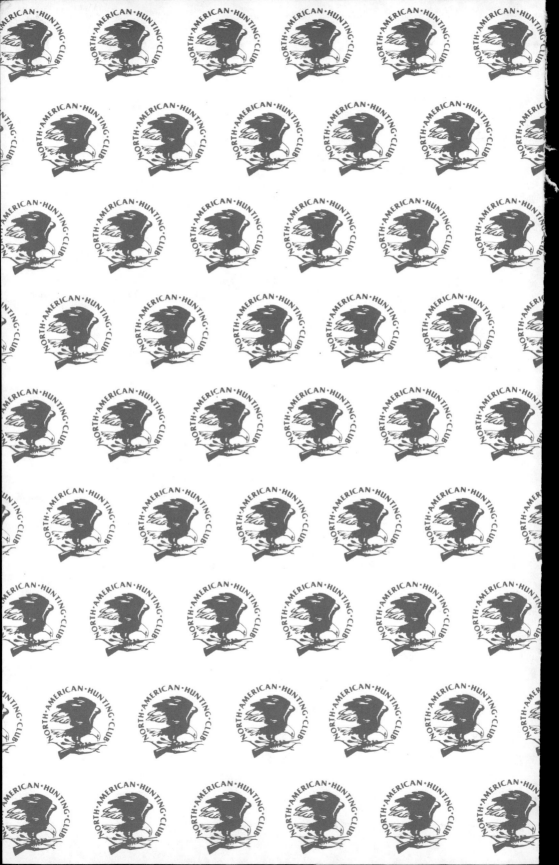